△  △  △

# The Third Striving

*Keith A. Buzzell*

△ △ △

© 2014 Keith A. Buzzell
First edition: ISBN 978-0-9763579-5-7

Keith A. Buzzell
499 Upper Ridge Road
Bridgton, ME 04009 USA

Fifth Press
444 East 200 South
Salt Lake City, UT 84111 USA
www.fifthpress.org

Rights Reserved.
Parts of this book may be used, if you would kindly write to ask permission from the author or publisher. Responses to the content of this volume, via the author or editors/publisher are also welcome.

Cover: NASA Casini telescope, image of Saturn's rings and the planet Earth.

Frontispiece: Hubble, Stellar Genesis in the Southern Pinwheel provides the cosmic ground, and the images are a collaboration with Michael Hall, author, editors and Amy O'Donnell.

# Dedicated to the Spirit of Hadji-Asvatz-Troov

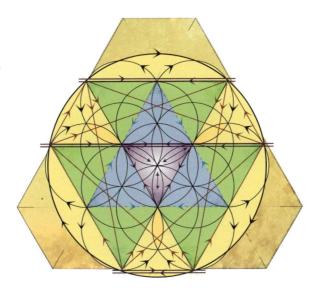

The Sixth Multiplication

In man the growth of conscience consists in the growth of the intellect and the growth of superior emotions which accompany it (aesthetic, religious, moral); in growing they become more intellectual and, at the same time, the intellect assimilates the emotions. "Spirituality" is a fusion of intellect with superior emotions.

G. I. Gurdjieff, "Meaning of Life," unpublished.

△  △  △

## Contents

PREFACE: *Stephen Aronson* .................................................................... *i*

AUTHOR'S INTRODUCTION — ESSENTIAL QUALIFICATION .................. 1
    Orbit of the Comet

THE SOLAR SYSTEM AS AN INDIVIDUAL ....................................................... 4
    The Third Brain ~ Mechanical/Being Instinct ~ Removal
    ~ The State of Consciousness ~ "…independent automatic moving …"
    ~ Paradox ~ Laws

TO STRIVE .................................................................................................. 11
    Definitions ~ Levels ~ Hierarchy

THE THIRD STRIVING:
    "…THE *CONSCIOUS* STRIVING TO KNOW EVER MORE AND MORE …"
    .............................................................................................................. 17

INTELLIGENCE AND CONSCIOUSNESS .................................................... 19
    Sensitivity, Density in the Atomic World ~ A Preposterous Proposal
    ~ Bonding Energies ~ Bonding Energies in the Food Octave
    ~ Intelligence and Consciousness of Food Undergoing Digestion

THE EMERGENCE OF A NERVOUS SYSTEM ............................................. 22
    Tetartocosmoses (multi-celled life-forms) ~ Mass to Non-mass —
    to Ionic Waves–to Nerve Fibers–to 'touch' — to the First Brain

THE RESONANCE OF LAW IN THE THREE OCTAVES OF FOOD ................. 26
    The Laws of Worlds 48–24–12 *Within* World 48 ~ Progressive
    Unbinding of Food Down to the Elementals ~ Entry of Air — $DO_{192}$
    and Absorption of Elementals *Into* the Body ~ Worlds *Within* Worlds
    ~ $FA_{96}$ and $RE_{96}$ ('hydrogen' 96) Processes ~ $H96$ to $H48$ Processes —
    Mass to Non-mass ~ Sound ~ Other Components of Air

RESONANT POSSIBILITIES ......................................................................... 32
    Qualifications of the $H12$ Category ~ $SI_{12}$ of Food—The 'Automatic'
    Attentions ~ $SOL_{12}$ of Air—The Attentions of Higher Emotional
    Center ~ Expressions of $FA_{24}$ toward $SOL_{12}$ ~ $MI_{12}$ of Impressions
    —The Attentions of Higher Intellectual Center

### Third Striving

Further Explorations in the Enneagrams
of Physical Food and Air..........................................................37
$LA_{24}$ and $SI_{12}$ of the Food Octave ~ Automatic Results—What Precedes
$LA_{24}$ ~ Buffers—or Not ~ $LA_{24}$ of Physical Food ~ $SI_{12}$ of Physical Food
~ Air–$MI_{48}$ of Air ~ $MI_{48}$–$FA_{24}$ Interval of Air ~ $SOL_{12}$ of Air

Influences of the First Conscious Shock.................................44

$DO_{48}$–$RE_{24}$–$MI_{12}$ of the Food of Impressions Enneagram...............50

The Second Conscious Shock...................................................52
$FA_6$ and $LA_6$ ~ In Sum

A Further Exploration of Law via
*A Symbol of the Cosmos and Its Laws*.........................................55
Apices of Triads

Times.........................................................................................59

The Lateral Octave and the Cycle of Life.................................63
From Three-brained to Kesdjan ~ The Collapse of the Lateral Octave

The Inner-Outer (psycho-physical) Nature
of the Laws of World-creation................................................66
Pre-Creation—the Principles of Three and Seven ~ Heropass

Symmetry and Creation...........................................................69

Laws of World 48....................................................................71
Food ~ Brained Beings ~ The Non-Mass Energies ~ Fields and Photons

Laws of World 24 in World 48.................................................75
Second Brain—Air Octave ~ Work in the Moment
~ The Lawful Hazard of the Passage from $MI_{48}$ to $FA_{24}$

Worlds 12 and 24 Laws in World 48........................................83
Summarizing Comment–Worlds 96, 48, 24, 12 and Six

Hazard......................................................................................87
Beelzebub's Aim ~ Indifference to Cosmic Law ~ Outside the Law
~ Egoism and Kundabuffer ~ 'Causes' of Kundabuffer ~ Egoism
~ Paradox ~ Work–Kundabuffer ~ Work–Egoism ~ A Personal
Reflection ~ The Exile ~ Singular Issue

Obyvatel...................................................................................97

The Paradox of Attention and Will Power:
'Seeing' and 'Doing'.................................................................101
The Separation of Divine Attributes in the Unfolding of Creation
~ Okidanokh and the Ray of Creation ~ The Role of Divine-Love
~ Wish and Love ~ Wish and Choice ~ The Ways

Consciousness — A Precondition for Love..........109
    A Lifetime of Effort

Instinctive Center/Sex Center: The Survival Triads..........111
    The Will to Be ~ The Role of Wish

Afterword
"... an organ like Kundabuffer ..."..........117
    fa and re $_{96}$ — sol and mi $_{48}$ ~ Removal and Destruction of Kundabuffer ~ A *New* Organ *Like* Kundabuffer ~ Role of Hassein ~ Consciousness and the Future ~ The Destruction of Egoism ~ Time

Involution?..........123

Glossary..........127

Reference — Recommended Reading..........131

Biography..........138

△ △ △

# Preface

Late one night, over thirty years ago, I was visiting with Dr. Keith Buzzell in his eighteenth century farm house deep in the forest of Western Maine. He was talking about the phenomenon of neural transmission. Long after midnight, I was on my feet, struggling to stay awake, not wanting to leave his company until he was ready to stop. The discovery of Gurdjieff's ideas, and Keith's connection with them, had appeared in miraculous fashion for me only a few months earlier. Both the ideas, and his understanding of them, were manna from heaven for my parched and starving Essence.

Since my youth I had been oriented to confirm for myself the truth of a Reality behind 'reality.' Given my intellectual predilections, I was attracted to the path of scientific discovery–or rather, the continually expanding edge of what was 'known.' It seemed that what I was searching for must lie in the darkness just beyond this always expanding circle of light. I loved the emotional thrill of walking up to the very edge of the known and staring into the abyss beyond. I also was aware that the depth of my longing to confirm the existence of this suspected Reality made me vulnerable to suggestibility, so I relied on my intellectual mind and avoided trusting my feelings. As a result, even when faced with inexplicable experiences, my formatory mind would intervene and tell me that since my experiences were 'subjective', therefore, I could not use them for verification.

Then, one night in April, 1982, at age 39, I experienced, what I can only describe as the singular 'vision' I have ever had in my life. Without going into detail, this experience led me, within two weeks, to the discovery of the Gurdjieff Work, of which I had been totally unaware. I knew immediately I

# Third Striving

had come "home" and my formatory logic surrendered to the emotional truth of the situation. Shortly thereafter I made contact with Keith and entered a relationship which is now beginning its fourth decade.

And so, there he and I were thirty years ago, in the wee hours of the morning, in the stillness of the forest, exploring what was currently known about the flow of electricity in the brain. Keith was speaking about the process of a 'something' moving along the axon to flip sodium-potassium ions back and forth across the membrane, producing an ionic wave which, if sufficiently strong when entering the neuron body, would jump across the synapse to initiate another movement of the 'something' along the next axon. The factual materiality of this process was so incomprehensibly complex and intelligent that I saw it could, in no way, be 'accidental.' There was an emotional excitement in my chest and something began to shift. As he spoke, I was aware of my body struggling to stay awake and the effort of will to command it to do so. At the same time, I was following a picture in my mind of the traveling "nerve impulse." My mind focused on the synapse between two nerve cells. Then I saw it! There, in the empty space between the dendrites of one cell and the neighboring axon of the next cell, was proof my intellect had been unable to see, despite all its opportunities to do so. The space was 'empty.' *Nothing* was there, but *Everything* was there! Nothing could happen without including the space. The mystery of the laws and principles that underlay everything was in the middle, in the center, in the space between things. The source of everything was in the 'Nothing.' A tear rolled down my cheek. "Why am I crying?" I asked Keith. "The Truth is like that," he replied. He had shown me how to use and trust my intellect and avoid suggestibility. I saw how one could know without thinking thoughts.

In many Gurdjieff groups, the appropriate fear of 'wiseacring' seems to lead many group leaders to relegate any interests of the intellect expressed in group meetings to 'formatory' processes and place focus primarily on work on Being. Yet, Gurdjieff tells us that knowledge and experience must develop together to produce Understanding, and that Understanding is the greatest force we can have within ourselves. His own dual scientific and spiritual nature led him to advise, "Take the Wisdom of the East and the Knowledge of the West and then Seek." Gurdjieff placed enormous emphasis on the absolute necessity of development of Reason in relation to the Higher Being-body. Beelzebub's entire exile is to allow him the chance to develop his impetuous, immature Reason. The first chapter in *Beelzebub's Tales to His Grandson*[1] is "The Arousing of Thought." Gurdjieff wants us to *think* for ourselves, from our own experience, to confront one of our greatest weaknesses—suggestibility.

---

1 Gurdjieff, George Ivanovitch, *All and Everything/First Series*, "An Objectively Impartial Criticism of the Life of Man," or *Beelzebub's Tales to His Grandson* (Aurora: Two Rivers Press, 1993) an exact facsimile republication, of the first edition, as prepared for publication in English by the author, unrevised; or (New York: Penguin Arkana, 1999). Herein referenced as *Beelzebub's Tales, The Tales* or (BT), pp 3-50.

# PREFACE

In approaching his study of Gurdjieff's ideas, Keith blends his knowledge of medicine and science with his years of practical work on himself—to link East and West, science and spirit, in exactly the way Gurdjieff enjoined: *Man is in the Universe and the Universe is in Man*—as above, so below."[2] The scientific method of observation, experimentation and verification is the heart of Gurdjieff's work on Being. Only through our work on Being can the ideas become alive and practically useful. Keith recognizes that understanding the laws can lead to a direct experience of an intelligent Universe and our own small place in it, to the direct perception that "the difference between each of them and our common great Megalocosmos is only in scale."[3]

For Keith, what our scientists have discovered about ourselves and our Universe is so unfathomably complex and interconnected, both transcendent and immanent, that it is sufficient as proof of an unimaginable intelligence behind the pattern. The pattern follows Principles, Gurdjieff calls the "Laws." The Laws must precede the pattern. As the manifestation of the greatest organizing intelligence, the Laws point to their origin as the 'space' beyond what exists—the place of No-thing. In the world outside, science has led us to the edge of the No-thing, just beyond the moment of creation at the limit of the known Universe. Inside it has led us to the place where ongoing creation comes from No-thing, currently called the "quantum foam," out of which appear and disappear "particles" of energy which ultimately bind together to form all and everything that is. Most likely, these two frontiers are the same 'place.' In the middle is Consciousness, the place of *reception* and *interpretation*. As we seem to be consciousness itself, we are thus part of the mystery inside the No-thing. To explore the Laws emanating from the realm of No-thing, we must also go inside ourselves.

In choosing to explore the Laws, Dr. Buzzell focuses, in this volume, on the third striving: "the conscious striving to know ever more and more concerning the laws of World-creation and World-maintenance." To my delight he once again shows that the solution lies in the middle. Fulfillment of the first and second striving, work on oneself (body and feelings) and the fourth and fifth strivings, work for 'other' (God and all creatures), are dependent upon what makes them possible and weaves them together. To practically work on these four strivings necessitates understanding how things actually work, what we are doing, how to do it and the reason why we are striving in this way. This is the middle that connects the ends. This is the third striving, which must permeate all the others to effect anything real. This is the Reason-of-Understanding,[4] the appropriate aim for the gift of intellectual potential given to us as three-brained beings.

---

2 Trismegistus, Hermes, *The Emerald Tablet*.
3 Gurdjieff, *Beelzebub's Tales*, P 775.
4 Ibid., PP 1166-1172.

Gurdjieff calls a man with only Being—but *without* Understanding—a "stupid saint." In following the example of Beelzebub, we must develop our horns as well as our heart. In following the example of Keith Buzzell, we find an earthly model—a spiritual scientist dedicated only to the search for Truth. Gurdjieff, in *Beelzebub's Tales to His Grandson*, speaks about the necessity of such men for the Cosmic Order;

> "… in most cases concerning these questions, just these ordinary three-brained beings, who acquire information … exclusively only thanks to their being-Partkdolg-duty, are more competent than any of the Angels or Cherubim with their prepared Being, …"[5]

Keith Buzzell has played this role in my life. Through his writings, *may* he play this role for many into the future.

*Stephen Aronson*

If the second body succeeds in becoming crystallized in a man before his death, it can continue to live after the death of the physical body. The matter of this astral body, in its vibrations, corresponds to matter of the sun's emanation and is, theoretically, indestructible within the confines of the earth and its atmosphere. All the same, the duration of its life can be different. It can live a long time or its existence can end very quickly. This is because, like the first, the second body also has centers; it also lives and also receives impressions. And since it lacks sufficient experience and material of impressions it must, like a newborn baby, receive a certain education. Otherwise it is helpless and cannot exist independently, and very soon disintegrates like the physical body.[6]

---

5 Gurdjieff, *Beelzebub's Tales*, p 1160.
6 Ibid., *Views from the Real World*, p 224.

# The Third Striving

*Keith A. Buzzell*

Editors: John Amaral, Marlena Buzzell,
Michael Hall, Bonnie Phillips, Toddy Smyth
Fifth Press, Salt Lake City

"In short, the transmutation in themselves of an all-round understanding of the functioning of both these fundamental sacred laws conduces to this, that in the common presences of three-brained beings, data are crystallized for engendering that Divine property which it is indispensable for every normal three-brained being to have and which exists under the name of 'Semooniranoos'; of this your favorites have also an approximate representation, and they call it 'impartiality'.[I]

*G. I. Gurdjieff*

" ... through attention we are able to stand between the world of facts and the world of possibilities."[II]

*J. G. Bennett*

For those who are awake there is a single, common world, whereas in sleep each person turns aside into his own, private world.[III]

*Heraclitus*

But we can't just teach our children what we already know— we must also train them how to discover what is not yet known ... creativity: the unexpected insights that come into discovery only as we try and fail and try again. These insights emerge from the empty space of possibility, out of which comes Archimedes' Eureka! and James Watson's dream of the double helix, a sonnet or a sonata, King's dream of freedom and Mandela's vision of justice. The empty space is the birthplace of possibilities that don't yet exist, but might.[IV]

*J. Hunter*

# Author's Introduction

To inquire into and come to an understanding of Law is a responsibility for all people who practice and pursue this Work. It is required (but not enough) to carry out a variety of practices and to struggle, in one's inner world, toward a realization of Conscience. Beyond this, Gurdjieff calls on us to *consciously* come to Objective Reason, and this requires us to contemplate and actively mentate as best we can on the Laws which define the working of our World. Only when we *understand* the laws can we hope to properly utilize the energies of Okidanokh in the coating process of Kesdjan and Higher Being-body. In speaking of this, Gurdjieff noted, concerning the Omnipresent Okidanokh:

> "'... the possibilities for three-brained beings to perfect themselves and ultimately to blend with the Prime Cause of everything existing depends exclusively also on it.[1]

## Essential Qualification

In our study of the Laws there is an essential difference that is important to emphasize between the scientific approach to laws and Gurdjieff's approach to Objective Reason. The typical modern 'scientific' approach in the physical sciences involves the search for what are referred to as primary laws – laws which are precisely predictive in a given interaction (e.g., between photons, electrons, atoms, molecules or larger bodies). Most often these interactions are described in mathematical or abstract terms (e.g., $E=Mc^2$, $A^2+B^2=C^2$). An absolute essentiality of this type of scientific inquiry is that the experiments that are constructed to test a particular hypothesis are carried out in isolation; as many extraneous factors as possible are eliminated in order to focus on the specific interaction between entities. The result is a precise prediction of behaviors.

---

1 Gurdjieff, *Beelzebub's Tales*, p 1158.

Difficulties appeared when these formulaic approaches were applied to less well-controlled conditions. Quantum theory introduced a lawful indeterminacy or imprecision of measurement that resulted in a statistical understanding of physical law. Even with this modification, the enormous power and relative accuracy of the formulaic approach lies beneath the inventions of television, the internet and all means of electronic and power transmissions.

A second difficulty with formulaic 'law' is more specific with regard to our major concern. That concern derives from the fact that real-life processes (from the physical to the emotional and intellectual) never occur in isolation. There is no way to control the multiplicity of influences that enter into all events. This is exemplified in Gurdjieff's presentation on the nature of the Laws of Seven and Three (in the changing of the law such that all three Forces are open to outside influences and in the changing of certain intervals). It is in the nature of the MI–FA interval of all evolutional octaves that unpredictability will enter because it is not possible to know all potential influences that enter at this interval. It is here that the principles of chaos and complexity, which have been developed during recent decades, enter and have specific (and considerable) but unpredictable consequences. The "Butterfly effect,"[2] well researched over the past twenty years, is a precise example of the long-term, unpredictable consequences of extremely small influences, which enter at the MI–FA interval; this includes various processes, from the digestion of food to the long-term development of weather patterns.

Gurdjieff's emphasis on the changes in the Laws of Seven and Three leads to clear inferences that directly impact the development of Objective Reason. Life is a very messy, complex affair and the digestive process of food, air and impressions present a number of overlapping intervals that introduce further unpredictability and opportunities for reconciliation, which *require conscious choices* in the pursuit of Objective Reason. The need for a three-brained confrontation with influences coming from both our outer and inner worlds is a requirement for this pursuit.

The isolated and essentially unreal precision of mathematical 'law' is an 'echo' of the Autoegocratic[3] process where, in the end, nothing *real* can happen. The *Trogo*autoegocratic process introduces the dynamism of a self-feeding in which *absolute* predictabilities cannot exist. This principle (the Trogoautoegocratic[4]) is fundamental to our approach in the present text.

Gurdjieff immediately immerses us in this requirement, in the study of the unpredictabilities of laws, by placing before us the mythic image of the comet Kondoor colliding with the nascent Earth. In what way is this an expression of law? The resultant unbalancing of Earth, Moon and Anulios presents an image of a cosmically lawful process that is a defining event for the entirety of *Beelzebub's Tales*. Without it, there would have been no need

---

2 A cumulatively large effect that a very small natural force may produce over a period of time.
3 Gurdjieff, *Beelzebub's Tales*, pp 750-56.
4 Ibid., pp 748-62.

# Introduction—Qualification

for the implantation of Kundabuffer or for the resultant Transapalnian perturbations; those "calamities" or "'cataclysm[s] not according to law.'"[5]

Thus, a significant portion of the difficulties which so intimately involve mankind derive, ultimately, from the collision of the comet Kondoor. We are confronted, immediately, with an expression or facet of cosmic law. How to begin to unravel this *lawful* manifestation?

## Orbit of the Comet

Gurdjieff introduces the cometary collision in this way:

> "And just this very comet, although it was then already concentrated, was actualizing its 'full path' for only the first time.
>
> "As certain competent Sacred Individuals also later confidentially explained to us, the line of the path of the said comet had to cross the line on which the path of that planet Earth also lay; but as a result of the *erroneous calculations* of a certain Sacred Individual concerned with the matters of World-creation and World-maintenance, the *time of the passing* of each of these concentrations through the point of intersection of the lines of their paths coincided, and owing to this error the planet Earth and the comet 'Kondoor' collided, and collided so violently that from this shock, as I have already told you, two large fragments were broken off from the planet Earth and flew into space.[6]

Note that it is an error in *timing* that constituted the error of the certain Sacred Individual. Time is an expression of Heptaparaparshinokh, the primary fundamental Law or Principle of process — one that HIS ENDLESSNESS had to *reconcile* in the creative process that led to the *unfolding* of our Universe.

Lawful *inexactitude* is an essential feature of the Law of Seven. Inexactitudes, such as the error in calculating the timing of the orbit of Kondoor, are an expression of this primary law.

Gurdjieff initiates the life of Earth with an accident of law, which is to become a defining and recurrent feature in *The Tales*. The *lawfulness* of this accident is a factor that each of us has to take in and digest, as an essential part of our life on Earth and is a primary reason why *striving to understand law* is an essential aspect of potent Work on ourselves.

To carry this expression of law into *The Tales*, Gurdjieff needed to create a *context;* a broad canvas on which he could portray, mythically, the involutional/evolutional motions inherent in the life of man. Gurdjieff sets the stage for this portrayal in his large-scale image of the solar system Ors.

---

5 Gurdjieff, *Beelzebub's Tales*, p 301 and throughout.
6 Ibid., p 82. (author's italics)

## The Solar System as an Individual

In previous books,[7] we have put forward a perspective that, metaphorically, looks on the solar system Ors as a three-brained individual. In this analogy, Earth is taken to be the third brain, the moon is taken to be the first brain and Anulios is taken to be the second brain. Mars becomes the Higher Emotional Center, and Saturn becomes the Higher Intellectual Center. The Six Descents of Beelzebub are descents into man's third brain. Each descent is a deeper penetration into the thinking (third) brain of three-brained beings, starting at the time of Atlantis (late Neolithic times) and progressing into the subconscious (the true consciousness) of the present. Beelzebub's 'home', while in this 'solar system', is on Mars (Higher Emotional Center) and it is on Mars that the Teskooano is established in order to *observe* activities on Earth (and on other 'planets' of the solar system). This establishes the site of real self-observation (from Higher Emotional Center). From Mars, Beelzebub visits Saturn (Higher Intellectual Center) where his "essence-friend" Gornahoor Harharkh lives. A close resonance, between Beelzebub and Gornahoor Harharkh, is established via the "'Kesdjanian-result-outside-of-me'," (*BT*, p 1152) namely, Gornahoor Rakhoorkh. This relationship becomes of great importance to our understanding of the *natural* resonance ("Kesdjanian" and Conscience) between Beelzebub's Higher Reason and the mature development of Higher Intellectual Center (Gornahoor Rakhoorkh).

The Sun, in the mythic image created by Gurdjieff, should be Real I but, because of the present state of three-brained beings, it is not the warm and radiant source of the wholeness/oneness of the individual but is, in reality, "… more covered with ice than the surface of what they call their 'North Pole.'"[8]—a powerful image of man's present mechanical, dependent status. Also, a humorous and, perhaps, cynical note, is found in the etymology of "Ors," which means "buttocks or arse end."[9]

### The Third Brain

What could Gurdjieff be referring to in his emphasis on the dominance of the third brain (planet Earth)? It is dominant not only in size (being the "fundamental piece") but also in its having to be the source of askokin for its detached fragments. He presents this important differentiation in this way:

> "Therefore the Most High Commission decided to take certain measures to avoid this eventuality.
>
> "And they resolved that the best measure in the given case would be that the fundamental piece, namely, the planet Earth, should constantly send to its detached fragments, for their maintenance, the sacred vibrations 'askokin.'[10]

---

7  Buzzell, *Gurdjieff's Whim*, (Salt Lake City: Fifth Press, 2012), pp 37-43, Mars as Higher Emotional Center and Saturn as the Higher Intellectual Center.
8  Gurdjieff, *Beelzebub's Tales*, p 135.
9  from Greek–Claiborne, Robert, *The Roots of English*, (TimesBooks, 1989).
10 Gurdjieff, *Beelzebub's Tales*, p 84.

It is our understanding that "askokin" is a reference to the foundational initiation of *experience*. The dominance of the third brain, as the initiator of all action into the world, is true for *all* brained beings. Even frogs, when their outer layer of brain tissue that will evolve into the third brain (neocortex) is removed, fail to initiate any 'motion' out into the external world. This initiation of action is the primary *source* of all *experience* (askokin). All brained beings evolve with this dominance of 'initiation' as a primary aspect of the third brain. The third brain is, thus, the functional and perceptual origin of a three-brained being's experience and this experience *feeds* the Moon (the physical body) and Anulios (the emotions). This explains the dominance in size of the image of Earth.

The reference to the outer layer (the incipient third brain) of a frog's brain raises another important question–that of the nature of a three-brained being. One could ask, "Are all creatures who have *independent automatic moving on the surface of planets* three-brained beings?" Neurophysiologic studies of the evolution of the central nervous system emphasize that centralized neural processes simultaneously develop with respect to: the organ systems within the body, the musculoskeletal system that moves the body, and the sensory systems that feed a central activation center (that commits the creature to action—into "independent automatic moving"). By those criteria, *all* brained beings are, by definition, 'three-brained'—having aspects that deal with the inside world, outside world and commitment into action.

Without "independent automatic moving" (the *action*) on the surface of planets, there would be *no* life experience. Included, in the nature of askokin, are the experiences of emotion and thought (Abrustdonis and Helkdonis) that must be *consciously separated from* the entirety of life's experience in order to assist the coating process of the Higher Bodies.

Gurdjieff differentiates *man* from other three-brained beings by referring to them as biped (walking upright on two legs) who have the potential to come to Objective Reason because of the intervention of the Divine Attention. This qualification of "biped" would apply only to three-brained beings of Earth and not to three-brained beings of all planets of the Universe.

## Mechanical and Being Instinct

The 'beginning spiritualization' of three-brained beings (*BT*, pp 86-88) appears to be a reference to the early appearance of *conscious experience*. Gurdjieff speaks of it in these ways:

> "But afterwards, just in the period when they also, as it proceeds on other similar planets of our great Universe, were beginning gradually to be spiritualized by what is called 'being instinct,' just then, unfortunately for them, there befell a misfortune which was unforeseen from Above and most grievous for them."[11]   *and* ...

---

11  Gurdjieff, *Beelzebub's Tales*, p 86.

# Third Striving

"And of course there began gradually to be crystallized in the three-brained beings there the corresponding data for the acquisition of objective Reason.

"In short, on this planet also everything had then already begun to proceed in the usual normal order.

"And therefore, my boy, if the Most High Commission under the supreme direction of the same Archangel Sakaki had not, at the end of a year, gone there again, perhaps all the subsequent misunderstandings connected with the three-brained beings arising on that ill-fated planet might not have occurred.[12]   *and ...*

"You must know that by the time of this second descent of the Most High Commission, there had already gradually been engendered in them—as is proper to three-brained beings—what is called 'mechanical instinct.'

"The sacred members of this Most High Commission then reasoned that if the said mechanical instinct in these biped three-brained beings of that planet should develop towards the attainment of Objective Reason—as usually occurs everywhere among three-brained beings—then it might quite possibly happen that they would prematurely comprehend the real cause of their arising and existence and make a great deal of trouble; it might happen that having understood the reason for their arising, namely, that by their existence they should maintain the detached fragments of their planet, and being convinced of this their slavery to circumstances utterly foreign to them, they would be unwilling to continue their existence and would on principle destroy themselves.

"So, my boy, in view of this the Most High Commission then decided among other things provisionally to implant into the common presences of the three-brained beings there a special organ with a property such that, first, they should perceive reality *topsy-turvy* and, secondly, that every repeated impression from outside should crystallize in them data which would engender factors for evoking in them *sensations of 'pleasure'* and *'enjoyment.'*

"And then, in fact, with the help of the Chief-Common-Universal-Arch-Chemist-Physicist Angel Looisos, who was also among the members of this Most High Commission, they caused to grow in the three-brained beings there, in a special way, at the base of their spinal column, at the root of their tail—which they also, at that time, still had, and which part of their common presences furthermore still had its normal exterior expressing the, so to say, 'fullness-of-its-inner-significance'— a 'something' which assisted the arising of the said properties in them.[13]

---

12  Gurdjieff, *Beelzebub's Tales*, p 87.
13  Ibid., pp 88-89. (author's italics)

Note the following concerning these quotes:

△ In the first of these quotations, emphasis is placed on the misfortune that was unforeseen from Above. Is this another example of an accident in cosmic law?

△ The High Commission did *not* have to seek and receive sanction from HIS ENDLESSNESS to implant Kundabuffer. They *did* have to seek HIS ENDLESSNESS' sanction to initiate the Ilnosoparnian Process.[14] They are two different expressions of law: Ilnosoparno has its origin from World One while Kundabuffer has its origin from Worlds 12 and 24.

△ Gurdjieff has combined the more dominant role of the third brain (determined by the collision of Kondoor) with the *potential* for the attainment of Objective Reason which is dependent on the further development of the third brain. This further development is inferred from the appearance of "mechanical instinct"–a point which appears to be restated in Gurdjieff's presentation in the chapter "Purgatory" when he discusses the appearance of "independent automatic moving."

> "The point is that when the 'common-cosmic-harmonious-equilibrium' had become regularized and established in all those cosmoses of different scales, then in each of these Tetartocosmoses, i.e., in each separate 'relatively-independent-formation-of-the-aggregation-of-microcosmoses' which had its arising on the surface of the planets–the surrounding conditions on the surface of which accidentally began to correspond to certain data present in these cosmoses, owing to which they could exist for a certain period of time without what is called 'Seccruano,' i.e., without constant 'individual tension'–the possibility appeared of independent automatic moving from one place to another on the surface of the given planets.
>
> "And thereupon, when our COMMON FATHER ENDLESSNESS ascertained this automatic moving of theirs, there then arose for the first time in HIM the Divine Idea of making use of it as a help for HIMSELF in the administration of the enlarging World.[15]

Given the dominance of the third brain (in size) and the inferred development of Objective Reason *more rapidly* than was desirable, it appeared necessary to Higher Law to delay that development. The result was the implantation of Kundabuffer. When *reality* is defined strictly in terms of the presence and motions of bodies, and subjective experience is gauged in terms of pleasure and enjoyment, then daily life for a three-brained being is 'topsy turvy'. Little or no consideration is given to the *inner*, relational experiences that are the focus of the emotional center (Anulios). Also, there is *no focus* on

---

14  Gurdjieff, *Beelzebub's Tales*, P 84.
15  Ibid., P 762.

the attainment of Objective Reason. The following illustrations are precise descriptions of the circumstance described in *In Search*:[16]

Above, the arrow shows the mechanical flow of activation. Below, the illustration shows the flow from Consciousness and Will directing the body.

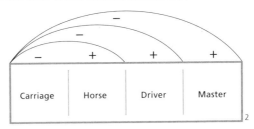

## Removal

When HIS ENDLESSNESS has the Divine Idea to make use of the "independent automatic moving" as a help in the administration of the enlarging world, the conditions for the coating process of Kesdjan and Higher Being-body enter and are then discussed at some length (*BT*, pp 762-65). We understand this as the entry of the *first conscious shock*, a distinct and remarkable application of law. With this development toward Objective Reason, the Air and Impressions Octaves of digestion can continue their processes – *although* the mechanical, *non*-conscious Food Octave *continues* to $SI_{12}$, and the Air Octave continues its $DO_{192}-RE_{96}-MI_{48}$ flow. These mechanical steps represent the *consequences* of the organ Kundabuffer. The *primacy* of the *automaton* has been *removed* from lawful significance but, because these automatic steps must continue, their consequences remain as part of the daily life of all three-brained beings. We can be *free* of Kundabuffer, but only when the first conscious shock is present and, over time, becomes a constant resource.

## The State of Consciousness

One further qualification of the third brain is important to note. Only via the third brain can man come to *consciousness* of himself and of his functional expressions (in images). The first (instinctive) and second (mechanical emotional) brains lie *below* the level of consciousness possible for the third brain. What is possible is that the third brain can and does create *images* from the chemical and neural input which originate in the first and second brains. Gurdjieff is very careful to caution us regarding any conscious action that could interfere or qualify the natural function of these centers.

---

16 P. D. Ouspensky, *In Search of the Miraculous: Fragments of an Unknown Teaching*, (San Diego: Harvest/HBJ Book, 2001) pp 42, 93.

This observation also helps to focus on the functional expression of the Food ($DO_{768}$ to $SI_{12}$) and Air ($DO_{192}$–$MI_{48}$) Octaves as the persistence of the *consequences* of the organ Kundabuffer. They are present in all of us (and *must* be for our survival) but should *not* be determining factors in the *conscious life* that begins and is maintained by the first conscious shock. Still and all, a significant part of our Work is in the observation of, and separation from these *automatic* functions of the body. In this way, we can come to understand the lawful utilization of the energies of Okidanokh for the coating process of Kesdjan and Higher Being-body.

### " ... independent automatic moving ... "

One of the most extraordinary events in the unfolding of the Lateral Octave of life was the appearance of "independent automatic moving from one place to another on the surface of the given planets." (*BT*, P 762)

In the Earth's oceans, *life* had come to self-activated motion long before the earliest creatures ventured onto the land. When independent moving on the surface began to take place, millions of years ago, it became possible then to trace the evolutionary development of *independently* moving limbs (rather than fins) and a respiratory system that could take in air as a true atmospheric substance and extract energy-giving oxygen and other substances.

Gurdjieff places *primordial* emphasis on the appearance of "independent automatic moving from one place to another on the surface of the given planets." All of man's possibilities derive from this momentous event and it is imperative that we enquire into why he understood this to be of such significance. The fact that he has HIS ENDLESSNESS re-enter the Megalocosmos with HIS Divine Attention and WHO then proceeds to elaborate the potential coating process of Kesdjan and Higher Being-body, gives emphasis to the importance Gurdjieff placed on the possibilities of "independent automatic moving."

### Paradox

How can anything be *independent* and *automatic* at the same time? This is a strange blending of what appear to be opposites. And why should this capacity be so important when it occurs "on the surface" of planets? Gurdjieff further appears to have qualified the possible appearance and development of Objective Reason by restricting his comments to *biped* three-brained beings of Earth. The appearance of the great toe, the freeing of the hands, the increase in lung volume (which greatly enlarges the input to the Air Octave), the differentiation of the larynx (making speech possible) and the massive enlargement of the third brain, were necessary developments on the road to the possible development of Objective Reason. Gurdjieff restricts this possibility by combining *conscious* ("independent") experience with *unconscious* automaticities (the automaton–the physical body and its instinctive center functions).

A portion of the mammalian life-forms *returned* to the ocean and we see these now in the population of whales, dolphins and other mammalian forms. Their limbs returned to the form of fins but they developed true aspects of family/relational life and have developed complex and subtle means of communication. They demonstrate considerable intelligence and significant evidence of 'self-awareness/self-recognition'[17]—learning in ways that are quite similar to the three-brained beings who walk on the surface of the planet. It is our understanding that they show intellectual and emotional features that are remarkably similar to ours and that they are considerably beyond the development of other mammalian species.

The same could be said of certain species of birds (notably, crows and ravens), who exhibit remarkable learning abilities and reasoning capacities. It is for these remarkable demonstrations of intelligence and rich relational life that we assign special triads of law in the Lateral Octave to mammals who have returned to the ocean and to certain species of birds (see illustration 13, p 59). Their placement infers a certain degree of Kesdjanian development and of Objective Reason that Gurdjieff recognized (as in the "raven" image of the beings of Saturn).

As remarkable as are these species of mammals (moving *independently* in the ocean) and those moving independently through the air, they were unable, in their third brain development, to come to the reality of an independent consciousness that could contemplate the laws of life's purpose and possibilities.

Man is able to walk on the land, swim in the ocean and, in recent years, to 'fly' (utilizing his intelligence) through the air. The abstracting capacities of his third brain can move *independently* of his physical existence and *independently view* his automatic functions and *study the lawfulnesses* that underpin his physical world and the Kesdjanian world of real relationship. In potential, he can become a unique, creative force in his world.

## Laws

In these opening segments, we have tried to emphasize the critical importance of the Third Striving—to comprehend the Laws (the Principles) of World-creation and World-maintenance. In the body of this book, we will focus on efforts to understand the laws which are operative in the digestive Octaves of Food, Air and Impressions. To be kept in mind is the unpredictability (the hazard) that lawfully enters each consideration of the digestive process. Only by this kind of effort, to understand more and more, will we fulfill the potential of coming to Objective Reason.

---

17  Reiss, Diana. *The Dolphin in the Mirror*, (Barnes & Noble, 2011).

## To Strive

"The first striving: to have in their ordinary being-existence everything satisfying and really necessary for their planetary body.

"The second striving: to have a constant and unflagging instinctive need for self-perfection in the sense of being.

"*The third: the conscious striving to know ever more and more concerning the laws of World-creation and World-maintenance.*

"The fourth: the striving from the beginning of their existence to pay for their arising and their individuality as quickly as possible, in order afterwards to be free to lighten as much as possible the Sorrow of our COMMON FATHER.

"And the fifth: the striving always to assist the most rapid perfecting of other beings, both those similar to oneself and those of other forms, up to the degree of the sacred 'Martfotai' that is up to the degree of self-individuality.[18]

△ What is a law?

△ More specifically, how is the expression "laws of World-creation and World-maintenance" to be understood?

△ Why is this pursuit of such importance that Gurdjieff would identify it as a fundamental striving?

### Definition(s)[19]

"Law" is a general term, having different nuances of meaning in a variety of contexts. We list here a number of the common contexts:

~A rule of conduct, recognized by custom or decreed by formal enactment, considered by a community, nation or other authoritatively constituted group as binding upon its members,

~Divine will, command or precept, especially as expressed in the Scriptures; also a body or system of rules having such divine origin,

~A rule of conduct, moral principle, etc., derived from a generally recognized concept of universal justice,

~Any generally accepted rule, procedure, or principle governing a specified area of conduct, field of activity, body of knowledge,

~In science and philosophy, a formal statement of the manner or order in which a set of natural phenomena occur under certain conditions,

From our perspective, there are resonances between each of these definitions and Gurdjieff's term "laws of World-creation and World-maintenance." The reasons for this are threefold:

1) Laws of World 48 concern, primarily, the physical world, the world of bodies and their motions. Modern science is focused on this world and has

---

18  Gurdjieff, *Beelzebub's Tales*, p 386. (author's italics)
19  Webster's Collegiate Dictionary.

produced many 'formal statements' of great accuracy which concern natural (physical) phenomena. In the past 150 years, various scientific disciplines have also 'discovered' rules that accurately describe phenomena in the biochemical (atomic-molecular) and electromagnetic fields. Investigations of the electromagnetic phenomena taking place in the brain have expanded a great deal in recent years, although there remain major questions (e.g., the nature of consciousness and of image formation) for which there are no present confirmable 'lawfulnesses'.

2) As a result of deeper investigations of physical phenomena in the 18th–19th centuries, the world of atomic-ionic-molecular interactions (World 24) was entered and, quite rapidly, many 'discoveries' of lawfulnesses took place. The fields of inorganic and organic chemistry were rapidly explored and found to contain a remarkably varied arena of great potentiality in terms of understanding the lawful processes taking place in the 'atmospheric' world of the physical body. The discovery, utilization and, eventually, synthesis of numerous hormones, neuropeptides, vitamins and physiologically active substances such as antibiotics, vaccines and anticancer agents has followed. At each step, various 'laws' of biological processes have been found that have great impact on our physical, emotional and intellectual behaviors.

Further investigations revealed the vast arena of relationships, of shared emotional states and of the lawful conflicts resulting from conscious and unconscious feelings that concern all self-other circumstances. The fields of psychology, psychiatry and neurology developed rapidly during the 20th century and many behaviors and chemical syndromes have been carefully described and a number of 'lawful' relationships have been discovered. A great many unanswered questions remain, in particular, questions which concern levels of consciousness and degrees of self-awareness.

Gurdjieff's differentiation of the second and third state of consciousness and their lawful significances still remains essentially unexplored by modern psychology/psychiatry.

3) Laws that concern life and man's possibilities and purposes (World 12) have found expression, via the Great Traditions and in certain of the major philosophies that have appeared. These 'laws' variably claim divine or Higher World origins and, because they are 'edicts' (in the sense that they are not arguable), they have an absolute character to them. Human reason, at its present level of development, can only endorse and follow, or disagree and pursue other 'laws' of purpose and meaning. Here, there are also historical examples of "Hasnamussian" claims regarding man's purpose and possibilities that have the creator's egoism at their core.

### Levels

Outlined above are at least three levels of 'lawfulnesses' having quite distinct frames of reference within Gurdjieff's presentation regarding the Ray of Creation. Listed are 1) phenomena of the physical (material) world; the world of bodies and their motions. These phenomena overlap and blend into the ionic-atomic-molecular world of the interiority of the body and of the water and atmosphere of Earth. At the second level, 2) are phenomena that concern the emotions (feelings) and inner sensations that take place automatically within living creatures. The third level 3) is of abstraction, a capacity fully developed only in three-brained beings. In addition to eventually addressing such questions as the meaning and purpose of life, this power of abstraction is first applied to communication (language–oral and written) and gradually applied to formal (primarily mathematical) descriptions of the phenomena taking place in 1) and 2). The questions regarding life's purpose form a separate category of abstraction.

## Hierarchy

We consider that the three octaves of digestion (Food, Air and Impressions) are separate but integrated expressions of the laws of World 48 (Food), the laws of World 24 (Air) and the laws of World 12 (Impressions). All of these laws are to be included in Gurdjieff's Laws of World-creation and World-maintenance. The foregoing material is an elaboration of that concept.

> ... scientific observation is impossible without pre-existing knowledge about what to look at, what to look for, how to look, and how to interpret what one sees. And he would explain that, therefore, theory has to come first. It has to be conjectured, not derived.[20]

The following two pages illustrate:
△ the change in the functioning of the two fundamental, sacred laws that resulted in the creation of the Universe, according to the chapter "Purgatory" in *Beelzebub's Tales*, and
△ enneagrams, both in an idealized form, and in a form which appears in the author's conception and elaboration of a symbol, referred to as *"A Symbol of the Cosmos and Its Laws."*

△   △   △

---

20 Deutsche, David, *The Beginning of Infinity*, (New York: Penguin Books), 2011, P 403.

---

ENDNOTES PAGE VI
 I Gurdjieff, *Beelzebub's Tales*, P 756.
 II Bennett, *Making a Soul, Human Destiny and the Debt of Our Existence*, (Bennett Books: Santa Fe, 1995), P 57.
 III Hericlitus
 IV John Hunter, *World Peace and Other 4th-Grade Achievments*, P 4.

" ... they become capable of becoming aware of the genuine corresponding place for themselves in these common-cosmic actualizations.

"In short, the transmutation in themselves of an all-round understanding of the functioning of both these fundamental sacred laws conduces to this, that in the common presences of three-brained beings, data are crystallized for engendering that Divine property which it is indispensable for every normal three-brained being to have and which exists under the name of 'Semooniranoos'; of this your favorites have also an approximate representation, and they call it 'impartiality'.
(BT, P 755-56)

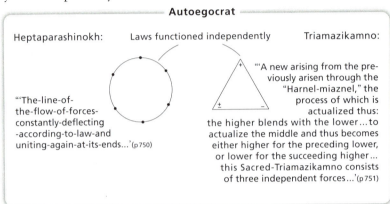

" ... our ALL-MAINTAINING ENDLESSNESS decided to change the principle of the system of the functionings of both of these fundamental sacred laws, and, namely, HE decided to make their independent functioning dependent on forces coming from outside.
(BT, P 752-53)

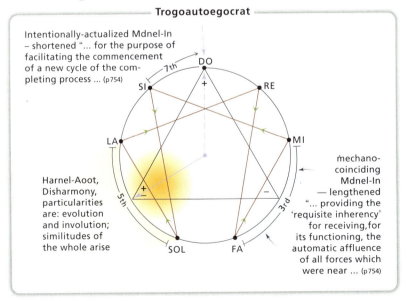

# Third Striving

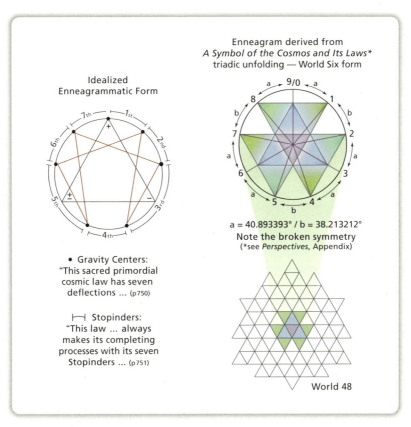

"I repeat, my boy: Try very hard to understand everything that will relate to both these fundamental cosmic sacred laws, since knowledge of these sacred laws, particularly knowledge relating to the particularities of the sacred Heptaparaparshinokh, will help you in the future to understand very easily and very well all the second-grade and third-grade laws of World-creation and World-existence. Likewise, an all-round awareness of everything concerning these sacred laws also conduces, in general, to this, that three-brained beings irrespective of the form of their exterior coating, by becoming capable in the presence of all cosmic factors not depending on them and arising round about them—both the personally favorable as well as the unfavorable—of pondering on the sense of existence, acquire data for the elucidation and reconciliation in themselves of that, what is called, 'individual collision' which often arises, in general, in three-brained beings from the contradiction between the concrete results flowing from the processes of all the cosmic laws and the results presupposed and even quite surely expected by their what is called 'sane-logic'; and thus, correctly evaluating the essential significance of their own presence, they become capable of becoming aware of the genuine corresponding place for themselves in these common-cosmic actualizations.

(BT, pp 755-56)

But the sea change in the values and patterns of thinking of a whole community of thinkers, which brought about a sustained and accelerating creation of knowledge, happened only once in history, with the Enlightenment and its scientific revolution. An entire political, moral, economic and intellectual culture–roughly what is now called 'the West'–grew around the values entailed by the quest for good explanations, such as tolerance of dissent, openness to change, distrust of dogmatism and authority, and the aspiration to progress both by individuals and for the culture as a whole.[I]   D. Deutsche

Everything is governed by law – which is very simple. I have shown you how the law works outside; now you can find out how it works in you. In accordance with the law, you can follow either the law of evolution or the law of involution. You must put the outside law inside.[II]   G. I. Gurdjieff

The foregoing might suggest that all semi-independent entities, from subatomic particles to galaxies, partake in some way in consciousness, and have some kind of inner life. Some believe this, but no one would attribute to molecules or cells the kind of awareness we have. Is it a matter of degree, or is there a threshold that makes possible the kind of inner world we are privileged to inhabit? One view is that it is the development in us of the capacity for abstract and symbolic thought, that in harmonious combination with sensations and emotions, makes it possible for us to resonate with the full reality of the universe.[III]   D. Deutsche

… When a great deal of fine matter accumulates in a man, there comes a moment when a new body can form and crystallize in him: the do of a new octave, a higher octave. This body, often called astral, can only be formed from this special matter and cannot come into being unconsciously. In ordinary conditions, this matter may be produced in the organism, but is used and thrown out.[VI]

G. I. Gurdjieff

ENDNOTES, PAGE 114

# The Third Striving: — "... the *conscious* striving to know ever more and more ..."

One way of characterizing all five strivings would be as a life-long, never-ending enterprise. There are several reasons why we choose to emphasize the third striving in this exploration:

△ The placement of the third striving at the midpoint of the five is significant because it lies at the balance point. The first two strivings are focused on personal Work, and the last two on payment and assistance to HIS ENDLESSNESS and all the other results of HIS labors. The first two strivings are, in a sense, preparatory for the last two; namely, meeting personal responsibilities toward the body and the Being prior to commitment beyond the self. The capacity of that commitment beyond oneself is dependent upon the understanding of "the laws of World-creation and World-maintenance," hence its placement at the balance point.

△ Great and continuing effort has been made by the various Gurdjieff Work groups to provide the means (via Gurdjieff's writings, his music, group meetings, Movements and Sacred Dances, exercises and the example of the 'tutors') for individuals to undertake the strivings. These means also assist individuals in their efforts to begin to understand the laws of World-creation and World-maintenance as they apply to the inner (psycho-spiritual) world of man. Here the ancient precept of "As above, so below" is applicable, as is Gurdjieff's statement that the growth of the Kesdjan and the Higher Being-body is a "... material process completely analogous to the growth of the physical body."¹ Impartial and prolonged self-observation begin the process of learning about the laws of the inner world. Over time, we 'see' our mechanical and negative manifestations and the contributions to that state which derive from our sensations, feelings and thoughts. These observations, by themselves, do not bring transformation. We do not become a different individual on the basis of these 'seeings'. We have not seen far enough into the laws. We have not *yet* seen the requirements of law that open to the possibility of real choice and decision.

△ One uniqueness of the Gurdjieff teaching is his incorporation of Western science as an integral contributor to the coating process of the Kesdjan and Higher Being-bodies. Understanding of the laws of World-creation and World-maintenance in the broadest sense is critical to that process. The complex lawfulnesses involved in our cellular and bodily physiology are an important aspect of this pursuit, as are the laws governing processes taking place on the surface and in the atmosphere of Earth. The fields of both subatomic physics and astronomical phenomena provide opportunities to learn about the fundamental principles of law at all levels of our Universe.

Impartiality, automaticity and hazards are operative in all of these processes; greatly assisting our understanding, especially of those processes that are operative in the Air and Impressions Octaves of digestion. Deep study of these laws makes it possible to avoid the 'dilemma' of the Toof-Nef-Tef of Mars (who has great wish to serve his people but does not know what to do —because he does not understand the laws of Higher Worlds) and to make appropriate decisions around choices which are consciously made. To fulfill the *fourth* and *fifth strivings* fully — we need, in a fundamental way, an understanding of the laws of Worlds 12–24–48 and 96.

> ... When I begin to think and study impartially, I find that religion and science are both right, in spite of the fact that they are opposed to one another. I discover a small mistake. One side takes one subject; the other side, another. Or they study the same subject but from different angles; or one studies the causes, the other the effects of the same phenomenon, and so they never meet. But both are right, for both are based on laws that are mathematically exact. If we take only the result, we shall never understand in what the difference consists.²

This exploration is both rather long and complex because it must take up exceedingly subtle and diverse processes. The many illustrations that the reader will come upon throughout this exploration were developed as an aid to the navigation of this difficult material. We strongly recommend that the reader make frequent use of these illustrations to orient and organize her/his perspective.

---

1 Ouspensky, *In Search*, P 180.
2 Gurdjieff, *Views from the Real World*, (New York: Dutton, 1973) P 200.

## Intelligence and Consciousness

"So far," he said, "we have looked upon the 'table of hydrogens' as a table of vibrations and of the densities of matter which are in an inverse proportion to them. We must now realize that the density of vibrations and the density of matter express many other properties of matter. For instance, till now we have said nothing about the intelligence or the consciousness of matter. Meanwhile the speed of vibrations of a matter shows the degree of intelligence of the given matter. You must remember that there is nothing dead or inanimate in nature. Everything in its own way is alive, everything in its own way is intelligent and conscious. Only this consciousness and intelligence is expressed in a different way on different levels of being—that is, on different scales. But you must understand once and for all that nothing is dead or inanimate in nature, there are simply different degrees of animation and different scales.

"The 'table of hydrogens,' while serving to determine the density of matter and the speed of vibrations, serves at the same time to determine the degree of intelligence and consciousness ...."[3]

Consciousness and intelligence are, then, relative to the speed of vibrations and the density of matter. What could this mean relative to atoms—to molecules—to living bodies—to a brain?

### Sensitivity in the Atomic World

Even an atom (any member of the periodic table of elements) has a range of sensitivities. By its molecular structure it is given a positive (+) charge (varying in strength from one element to another) which creates a tiny but varied field around the nucleus. The electron (− charge) orbits the nucleus in a complex series of 'shells', determined by the field established by the nucleus. The electron orbitals establish a field—an 'awareness' of the same (−) and opposite charge (+), and this field determines the arena of possible interactions with other charged atoms and other energies (photonic and electromagnetic fields). This sensitivity could be termed awareness or consciousness and the potential for various interactions would be a measure of the 'intelligence' of the atom, (illustration 1, p 20).

### Density in the Atomic World

The internal environment of an atom is equally interesting and complex. Of first importance is that it is the coalescence of mass. A proton (the nucleus of a hydrogen atom) is the most dense object in the relatively low temperature/pressure world of planetary existence (Worlds 24–48) and of moons (World 96). Its mean lifetime (mathematically estimated) is greater than (>) $2.1^{1024}$

---

3 Ouspensky, *In Search*, p 317.

years![4] Paradoxically, the mass of a proton is attributed to the confinement of energy and not to a transmutation to an absolutely solid 'something'. The constituents of a proton (considered to be 3 partially charged quarks and the energy binding gluons)[5] 'orbit' each other in a seemingly 'eternal embrace'. According to modern theoretical considerations, the quarks contribute less than 5% to the total mass of the proton whereas the energy-bearing gluons comprise better than 95%. The state of affairs 'inside' a proton is clearly impossible for us to visualize as the component quarks and gluons 'dance' at phenomenal speeds around each other.

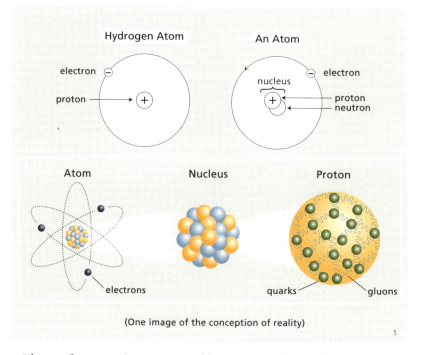

(One image of the conception of reality)

The confinement (meaning *unable to escape from*) of quarks and gluons in the nucleus of a proton is an absolutely permanent state of affairs in Worlds 24–48–96. It is only in higher regions of World 12 extending into World 6 that sufficient energy is available to 'unlock' the bonds that confine the quark gluon complex and which thereby leads to the release of that energy-of-confinement. The energy of confinement is enormous! We saw examples of this in the hydrogen bomb explosions in the 1950*s*, which clearly demonstrated that this level of energy release, while 'lawful' in World 12, is not a natural occurrence in any world below that of suns.

---

4  That is 2,100,000,000,000,000,000,000,000,000,000 years–far longer than the estimated age of the Universe!

5  The theories of quark/gluon dynamics are extremely complex, well beyond our ability to consider here.

## A Preposterous Proposal

The coalescence of mass, early in the unfolding of the creation of the Universe, is an absolutely critical event. The entirety of the Worlds of Suns, Planets and Moons (Worlds 12, 24, 48 and 96) would be impossible without a semi-permanent to permanent density to serve as a substrate *building block*. One could say that in the inner nature of the proton can be glimpsed the Negative Absolute — that state of near absolute inertia and resistance to change that can only be *entered and altered* by the extraordinary energy of the Creation itself (Positive Absolute).

In its mass aspect, the proton is nearly impenetrable and resistant to change. It is the densest state, in terms of vibration, that exists. If it did not have an electromagnetic positive (+) charge in its environment, it would be unable to interact with anything. Through that positive charge it is enabled to form a relationship with an electron (–) and this ability opens it to the enlarging world of atomic interactions.

The gradual creation of the atomic table of the elements involves the combining of protons and neutrons in lawfully permitted sequences. The process involves a portion of the intra-atomic (the strong force between protons and neutrons) energies but not the inner quark/gluon energies that define the individual proton and neutron. We mention the table of elements here to highlight the emergence of complex +, – (proton, electron) interactions that underpin the entirety of chemistry and the formation of combinations of elements into salts, metals, etc.. The entirety of Worlds 24, 48 and 96 unfold with this plethora of interactions between electron shells. Withal, it is the density of the proton that we point to in our effort to understand what Gurdjieff emphasizes in the density of vibrations and the density of matter.

## Bonding Energies

Binding the nucleus into a *one* is the strong nuclear force (one of the four fundamental universal forces with the weak nuclear force, gravity and the electromagnetic force). The spatial 'reach' of the strong force is very short, barely extending beyond the boundary of the nucleus. A portion of this force makes possible the joining together of protons and neutrons in the enlarging creative process of the atomic table of the elements.

The bonding energies beyond the nuclei of atoms derive primarily from the electromagnetic force (the + and –) of the proton and the electron. In Worlds 24, 48 and 96 the electromagnetic force is the primary determinant energy in the infinity of interactions (bondings and unbondings) that take place.[6] Gravity is the final bonding energy of the Universe; its attraction influences all mass and energy, both locally and extending throughout the dimensions of the Universe.

---

6 See "Gurdjieff's 'hydrogens,'" chapter 9 of *Perspectives* for a more complete discussion.

## Bonding Energies in the Food Octave

The bonding energies on the right half of the Three Foods enneagram (P 27), from $DO_{768}$ to $FA_{96}$, are chemical (electromagnetic) in nature. Higher (enzymatic) energies are needed to break/*open* the bonds of the complex proteins, carbohydrates and fats in $DO_{768}$ and these derive from the numerous activities at $FA_{96}$. The transformation from a mass-based process (electronic bonds) at $FA_{96}$ to a non-mass-based process at $SOL_{48}$ (ionic impulses) is a *major change* in the type of bonding that takes place. To be kept in mind is that it takes place automatically and in accordance with the laws of World 48.

## Intelligence and Consciousness of Food Undergoing Digestion

According to the earlier quotation from Gurdjieff, the diversity of matter and its speed of vibrations determine its consciousness and intelligence. Sensitivity to its surroundings and the versatility of possible responses to those surroundings would appear to be a relative measure of consciousness and intelligence. By those criteria, the unbonding taking place at $DO_{768}$ and $RE_{384}$ leads to greater possible interactions, and a lessening of the density of $DO_{768}$. This would then be an increase in consciousness (sensitivity to its environment) and intelligence (more opportunities of interaction). With each step, $DO_{768}$–$RE_{384}$–$MI_{192}$, the consciousness and intelligence increases, reaching its acme in the ionic (highly reactive) state at $FA_{96}$. A measure of that level of consciousness and intelligence is seen in the remarkable capacities of DNA and in the multitude of processes that maintain the physical body taking place at $FA_{96}$. It is our understanding that these processes take place under the 24 orders of law from World 24 that obtain within World 48. Even non-brained creatures (micro- and Tetartocosmoses) have this portion of the enneagram ($DO_{768}$ to $FA_{96}$), although with them it is stretched out to an entire enneagram, so it would have a different sequence of notes. The principle would remain the same: the transition to $SOL_{48}$ involves an exploration of the neural impulses which are the bedrock of a nervous system.

## THE EMERGENCE OF A NERVOUS SYSTEM

The appearance of a three-brained being is the culmination of a 'neural' journey that has encompassed well over six hundred million years! Here, we undertake an abbreviated tour along this journey, highlighting the lawful steps that led from the electromagnetic-ionic field influences of adjacent cells, to the earliest neural fibers, to the final appearance of a centralized nervous 'system'. This journey highlights the essentiality of the third striving.

### Tetartocosmoses (multi-celled life-forms)

Non-brained life-forms have been, and still are, extraordinarily successful in their persistence and diversification. In terms of the digestive octave of food, all of these multi-celled creatures follow the opening notes ($DO_{768}$–

$RE_{384}-MI_{192}-MI\text{-}FA$ *interval* $-FA_{96}$) of the Three Foods enneagram (P 27). Each of the life-forms has its own complete enneagrammatic form; therefore a note-to-note correspondence with the familiar enneagram is not present. Being able to digest food from $DO_{768}$ to $FA_{96}$ is adequate for multi-celled life, as the DNA within its cells can direct the elaboration of enzymes, hormones, ions, proteins, complex fats and carbohydrates with great efficiency. There is no need of a nervous system in Tetartocosmoses of this type, as $H96$ processes provide all the energies and forms required for persistence and reproduction. $RE_{96}$ of the Air Octave in non-brained life provides the ionic forms and patterns that make possible various expressions of action and vitality that greatly enable the physical structures of $FA_{96}$ in life's activities. Essential to note is that $H48$–$24$–$12$ substances *do* appear in Micro- and Tetartocosmoses but they are restricted to intracellular and intercellular influences. A separate *system* (a brain) does not occur in a host of multicellular creatures.

## Mass to Non-mass — to Ionic Waves – to Nerve Fibers – to 'Touch' — to the First Brain

How is it possible to see into the emergence of a non-mass-based process (one that relies on ionic waves, electromagnetic fields and photonic energies) from the world of atoms and molecules that results in brained life? We must look closely at the ionic state — utilized at $FA_{96}$ and $RE_{96}$. The attractive/repulsive (+ or –) forces inherent in the electron shell must be the basis of ionic waveforms (the essence of a neural impulses). The solution found by evolutionary trial and error began with specialized electrical signaling cells in multi-celled creatures. The cells accomplished this by adapting the mechanism of action potentials (ionic waves) which had been lawfully manifested earlier in Microcosmoses.

Positive (+) ions (calcium, sodium and potassium) have slight differences in charge because of the structure of their electron shells. If any two of these ions move across a cell membrane in opposite directions, a slight difference in electrical potential results. If these ions are arranged along the inner and outer membrane of the cell, and the channels through the membrane exist which permit the ions to move in or out across the membrane, then, if one channel suddenly opens (due to an adjacent electrical impulse), an electrical potential develops where the ions move in and out. This potential varies as a non-mass waveform which, if the ionic 'cross movement' (of calcium-sodium or potassium) spreads to successive channels, then an ionic waveform is propagated along the membrane. This ionic wave can function as a carrier of information or as an initiation of a chemical action within the cell.

Gradually, small conduction fibers (early neurons) appeared both within and between cells, greatly facilitating the chemical processes necessary for the maintenance of the organism. This process occupied millions of years.

During this early period of nerve fiber proliferation, a number of these fibers ended at the outer membrane of the cell. These fiber ends were sensitive to changes in the electrochemical environment on the surface, reporting changes in that environment and initiating responses. Thus, if a molecule appeared proximate to the outer cell wall that could be utilized by the cell as food, it could be 'recognized' by the nerve ending and a process was initiated that led to the absorption of the molecule.

If the proximate molecule was not 'identified' as food, then its presence could be registered, either as of no threat or as a threat to the biochemical integrity of the cell wall. Thus, the external senses had their beginning in a kind of 'touch'. Over much time, the sensitivity to energies along the external membrane diversified to include the registration of photonic energies (light) and sound vibrations. The entirety of the external senses of brained beings had their beginnings in this sensitive interface of the cell membrane via the gradual appearance of sensitive nerve endings.

Over millions of years, the nerve nets linking various cellular components of organisms expanded and diversified, sharing more and more data about the individual cell processes and coordinating their varied actions. Nerve fibers began to collect together, joined together by the third type of nerve fiber (the associative fibers) into an emerging 'system', which linked the inner/outer environments of the organism in 'instinctive' self-preservation patterns. We recognize these patterns as forming the survival triad of what is to become the first brain.

The incoming (sensory) and outgoing (motor) fibers became organized (because of its economy and efficiency) around a central core of associative fibers—leading to what is now called the spinal cord. At the apex of this cord, a dense matrix of associative fibers came gradually into being, with 'centers' controlling and monitoring the basic survival capacities (food intake, elimination, circulation, physical defense [external] and auto-immune defenses [internal]). All were carried on automatically under the electrochemical laws of World 48.

Over this extended period of time, multi-celled life overcame the mass/non-mass divide and developed mechanisms and processes that utilized the ionic waveform as a means to monitor (sensory) and direct (motor) a wide variety of large-scale cellular processes that concern survival. A primitive but highly organized instinctive center (or first brain) had coalesced–focused on the individual survival of the organism. It is at this time that " ... independent automatic moving ..."⁷ appeared.

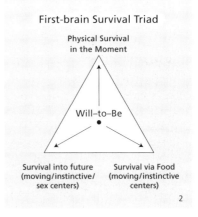

7  Gurdjieff, *Beelzebub's Tales*, p 762.

# RESONANCE—FOOD OCTAVES

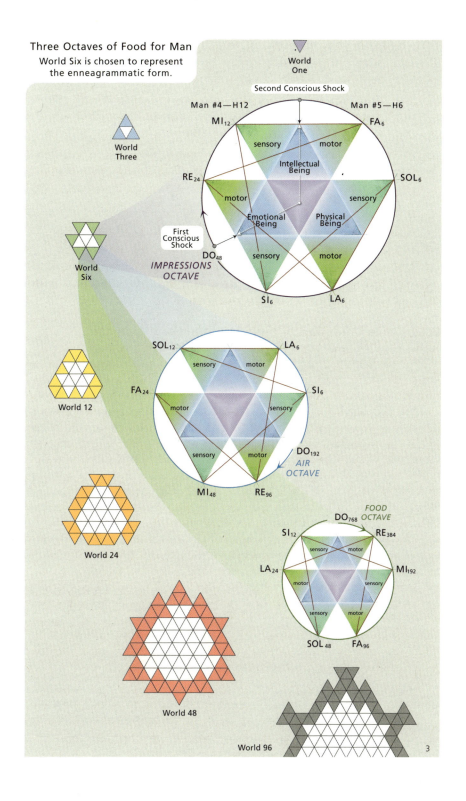

Three Octaves of Food for Man
World Six is chosen to represent the enneagrammatic form.

## The Resonance of Law in the Three Octaves of Food

It is interesting and essential to explore the resonance of law that exists in the three Evolutionary Octaves of Physical Food, Air and Impressions.

> " ... Inner growth, the growth of the inner bodies of man, the astral, the mental, and so on, is a material process completely analogous to the growth of the physical body."[8]

We have explored this analogy of lawfulness to some degree in previous chapters,[9] but we will go into considerably more detail in the present effort.

## Laws of Worlds 48—24—12 *Within* World 48[10]

Our first provisional assertions are that the ...

△ Food Octave ($DO_{768}$ to $SI_{12}$) is operative under the laws of World 48,
△ Air Octave ($DO_{192}$ to $LA_6$) is operative under the laws of World 24,
△ Impressions Octave ($DO_{48}$ to $FA_6$) is operative under the laws of World 12.

We will take up the action of the different World Laws as we explore the resonant notes and intervals of the three octaves.

## Progressive Unbinding of Food Down to the Elementals

In the Food Octave ($DO_{768} - SI_{12}$), we deal with the progression from the macromolecular materialities of raw food to the non-mass materialities of $SOL_{48}-LA_{24}-SI_{12}$. Each step is guided by the laws of World 48. From $DO_{768}$ through $FA_{96}$ our focus is on the bonding energies[11] that hold the macro- and micromolecules of proteins, fats and carbohydrates together, down to the level of amino acids and simple sugars and fats (the 'elementals' of this food). It is the action of digestive enzymes and the acidic and alkaline environment of the stomach and small intestine that makes this progressive unbinding possible–taking apart the large and smaller molecules until the elementals ($MI_{192}$) are the singular product. All of the uniqueness of the individual proteins, carbohydrates and fats (at $DO_{768}$), deriving from the unique DNA of the animals and plants that make up $DO_{768}$, is eliminated by the digestive process to $MI_{192}$. At this simplest of levels of the raw food, the process of absorption across the membrane of the intestine takes place–and the elementals *can enter* the physical body via the lymph and the blood.

Prior to $MI_{192}$ (the MI–FA interval), the food of $DO_{768}-RE_{384}-MI_{192}$ is *not in* the body (the digestive tube runs through the body but is not truly within it). This fact has important *resonances-of-law* in both the Air and Impressions Octaves. The $DO_{192}-RE_{96}-MI_{48}$ of Air takes place outside the

---

8  Ouspensky, *In Search*, p 180. (author's italics)
9  Buzzell, Keith, see the chapter "DO–RE–MI," *A New Conception of God*; (Salt Lake City: Fifth Press, 2012), pp 144-95.
10 Here we follow the elaboration of laws as given in *In Search*, pp 78-90, where the 48 laws of World 48 include 24 laws of World 24, 12 laws of World 12, 6 laws of World Six and three laws of World Three.
11 Chemically, there are three types of bonds: hydrogen, van der Waals and covalent. The bonds have quite varied strengths and means of expression.

# RESONANCE—FOOD OCTAVES

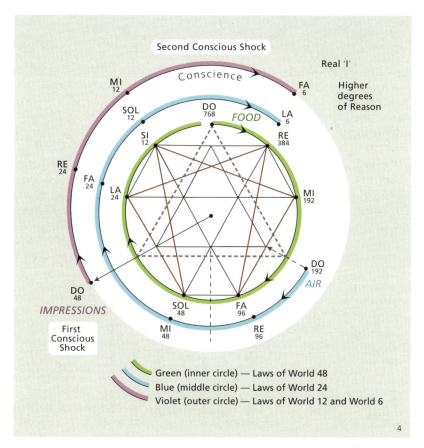

body (Kesdjan) to be served. The $DO_{48}$–$RE_{24}$–$MI_{12}$ of the Impressions Octave takes place outside of the body (Higher Being) which it will serve. In both instances, the elementals of the respective bodies are reached at MI.

### Entry of Air—$DO_{192}$ and Absorption of Elementals *Into* the Body

The absorption of the elementals and the entry of air (via the respiratory tract) are, in time, simultaneous, although separate, events. The absorption of the elementals is into the venous (and lymphaticovenous) circulation of the small intestine whereas the air enters the lung capillaries and the oxygenation of the blood changes the venous into arterial (oxygen containing) blood.

We are, then, at the entry point into $FA_{96}$. The elementals of food are transported into the cells of the body (a significant portion going first to the liver), and the oxygen becomes the fuel in the cellular process which leads to the production of ATP (the primary source of energy for all cellular processes). It is within the cells (under the guidance/control of the person's DNA) that the unique proteins and complex protein-carbohydrate-fat of that person's physical body are created. There are, literally, thousands of different substances created in this $FA_{96}$ process–all of them (the final proteinaceous

## Third Striving

products that are present in the tissues and organs of the body) serving for the maintenance of the physical body. All of these processes are 'governed' by laws of biochemistry, which are included in the laws of World 48. At the same time, *lawful inexactitudes* enter the $MI_{192}$–$FA_{96}$ interval, e.g., the $O_2$ content of the air, sound waves enter, as do molecular constituents like odors, pheromones, heat and humidity. *All* enter into the digestive processes and can have profound effects on the higher digestive steps of the Air Octave.

One unique resonance between $FA_{96}$ of Food and $RE_{96}$ of Air is emphasized here (which points to an important difference between RE and FA of all octaves). The protein-based substances created at $FA_{96}$ are unique to the individual body. This is because the DNA of each individual has unique features. This is the basis of tissue rejection which is so well known in organ transplantation. However, the active, enlivening substances (the hormones

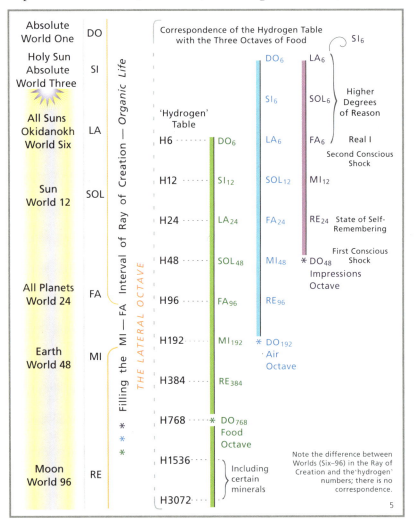

and neurotransmitters) are created by $RE_{96}$ processes, and these are not unique. They are shared by all three-brained beings, which is why the insulin, thyroid, adrenocortical, sexual and central nervous system hormones and neurotransmitters are transferable among all three-brained beings; they are identical substances. This demonstrates a unique feature of the Air Octave. We three-brained beings breathe the same air, create the same hormones and other enlivening substances, and, as a result, subjectively experience the same bevy of emotional states.

This is not true of the progressive steps of raw food ($DO_{768}$) in the Food Octave. Physically, we are each unique and different in a host of ways from each other and this difference is reflected in $LA_{24}$ (images) and $SI_{12}$ (attentions) of the digestion of food. Our individual Itoklanoz is also unique and creates the incredibly complex physical lives of each three-brained being.

All of the $FA_{96}$ and $RE_{96}$ processes take place automatically—ruled by rigorous lawfulnesses, which circumscribe all possibilities of manifestation. The same could be said of $SOL_{48}$ and $MI_{48}$. They derive from the macro- and micromolecular processes that occur under the laws of World 48 (the macromolecular processes that concern the structure of the body), and the laws of World 24 (the micromolecular and atomic/ionic processes that concern the actions and vitality of the body). The precise forms of the macromolecular, structural substances ($FA_{96}$) are determined by the unique DNA of the individual. The lawfulnesses are of World 48–centered on the need for all lifeforms to have a body, a physical presence. The micromolecular and atomic/ionic substances are not of the physical Earth but are 'atmospheric' in their nature. Hence, they are created under the laws of World 24, within World 48, and are not restricted to the physical body of the unique DNA. They are shared; they are identical substances that come into being at the earliest stages of the Kesdjanian (Air) Octave. The fact that they are shared by all three-brained beings is extremely important because it indicates that all subjective emotional states (feelings) that appear later in this octave *will be the same.*

> ' ... Try to put yourself in the position of others–they have the same significance as you; they suffer as you do, and, like you, they will die. Only if you always try to sense this significance until it becomes a habit whenever your attention rests on anyone, only then will you be able to assimilate the good part of air and have a real "I". Every man has wants and desires which are dear to him, and which he will lose at death.
>
> 'From realizing the significance of your neighbor when your attention rests on him, that he will die, pity for him and compassion towards him will arise in you, and finally you will love him; also, by doing this constantly, real faith, conscious faith, will arise in some part of you and spread to other parts, and you will have the possibility of knowing real happiness, because from this faith objective hope will arise–hope of a basis for continuation.'[12]

---

12  C. S. Nott, *Teachings of Gurdjieff*, (New York; Penguin, 1991), p 114.

## Worlds *Within* Worlds

The *first brain* (instinctive/moving/sex) carries on its functions under the laws of World 48, with its focus being on the maintenance and continuance of the physical body. The Food Octave ($DO_{768}$—$SI_{12}$) supports and expresses this lawfulness.

The *second brain* (emotional/feeling) carries on its functions under the laws of World 24 with its focus being on the shared, relational life of self/other. The Air Octave ($DO_{192}$—$LA_6$) supports and expresses this lawfulness.

The *third brain* (intellectual) carries on its functioning in accordance with the laws of World 12, with its focus being on the seeing, exploring and understanding of both the creative and maintaining laws of all Worlds. The Impressions Octave ($DO_{48}$—$FA_6$) supports and expresses this lawfulness.

Emphasis is placed here on the fact that, while the Kesdjan Body begins in the micromolecular-atomic/ionic world of the physical body ($DO_{192}$–$RE_{96}$), this is not its true environment–which is entered at $FA_{24}$. Kesdjan is a *wholly* different 'Body', with a vastly different nature, capacity and possibilities.

As Gurdjieff notes,

> "Now from such cosmic results, exactly similar forms began to be coated in their common presences, at first from the cosmic substances Mentekithzoin, i.e., from the substances transformed by the sun and by other planets of that solar system within the limits of which the given Tetartocosmoses had the place of their arising, and which cosmic substances reach every planet through the radiations of the said cosmic concentrations.
>
> "In this way, the common presences of certain Tetartocosmoses began beforehand to be composed of two different independent formations arisen from two entirely different cosmic sources, and these began to have a joint existence, *as if one were placed within the other*.[13]
>
> ...
>
> "As regards the second-being-body, namely, the body-Kesdjan, this body, being formed of radiations of other concentrations of Tritocosmoses and of the Sun itself of the given solar system, and having entered after the second process of the sacred Rascooarno into the sphere just mentioned, also begins gradually to decompose, and the crystallizations of which it is composed go in various ways into the sphere of its own primordial arisings.[14]

## $FA_{96}$ and $RE_{96}$ ('hydrogen' 96) Processes

The enormity of what takes place at the $H_{96}$ level is also to be emphasized. As noted earlier, there are thousands of macro- and micromolecules and ions created via the DNA-directed processes that take place here. The processes are never-ending, changing from one need to another, depending on life events taking place–in spaces and times that are incommensurate with the

---

13  Gurdjieff, *Beelzebub's Tales*, p 764. (author's italics)
14  Ibid., p 768.

spaces and times of the physical body's daily life. The entirety of our evolutional history is 'replayed' constantly, from Microcosmoses (one-celled) through Tetartocosmoses (multi-celled) and each of the levels of the three brains—a truly miraculous process![15] While the biochemical processes of $FA_{96}$ and $RE_{96}$ are carried out under the laws of World 48, it must be kept in mind that the *pattern*, the *ordering of the laws*, comes from the do (World 12) and si (World 24) of the Lateral Octave itself; the $SOL-FA$ of the Ray of Creation, identified on illustration 13, p 59 in this volume.

### H 96 to H 48 Processes — Mass to Non-mass

A unique feature of the intervals, $FA_{96}-SOL_{48}$ of Food and $RE_{96}-MI_{48}$ of Air, is that the mass-based substances of $FA_{96}$ and $RE_{96}$ undergo transformation to the non-mass-based substances (ionic wave forms) of $SOL_{48}$ and $MI_{48}$. These are the substrate 'substances' of all brains, the neural impulses (ionic wave forms) that initially provide the data that lead to the image formation that takes place at $LA_{24}$ of the Food Octave (and, with the first conscious shock, at $FA_{24}$ of Air and $RE_{24}$ of the Impressions Octave).

The neural impulses (the $H_{48}$ 'substances') produce data which reflect the results of the actions taking place in macro-/micromolecular, atomic/ionic processes, within the physical body. In a sense, each group of neural impulses represents a meaning; *a coalescence of data from the biochemical world*! From the coalescence of all the neural data, an image is created within the related electromagnetic fields of the brain, which is within the non-massed World 24.

### *Sound*

One remarkable feature of the $FA_{96}-SOL_{48}$ and $RE_{96}-MI_{48}$ intervals is the entry of sound. Sound waves are non-mass vibrations that derive from the vibrations of mass-based particles. They enter, in a sense, as 'higher' vibrations than mass but 'lower' vibrations than ionic waves. They are transformed in the ear to ionic waves and continue in the digestive octaves of food and air. Their varied origins are essential to keep in mind. These are sounds that originate in the material world—of oceans, mountains, wind, volcanoes, etc.. There are a multitude of sounds originating in life processes (from mosquitoes to gorillas) and most importantly in regard to possible 'higher' vibrations, from human beings: in speech, music and other human-originated sources.

### *Other Components of the Air*

There are a number of micromolecular substances (e.g., pheromones) deriving from other life-forms (both plant and animal) that enter the body via the air. Their functions in the body are not well understood. Ions of various atomic substances also enter via the air. Nitrogen (in gaseous, diatomic form) is an important pressure regulator within the atmosphere. Even photons (light) transit the air.

---

15  Brown, Jason, *The Self Embodying Mind*, forward, (Barrytown: Station Hill Press, 2002).

# Third Striving

△ △ △

## Resonant Possibilities

DO – RE of any evolutionary octave is a movement toward possibilities, toward an exploration of potential. It occurs in a context, or environment, that is totally different from the context of the DO itself although the DO sounds a note that, in its potential overtones and progression, contains *all* notes of the octave. $DO_{768}$ of Food moves to the watery environment of $RE_{384}$, beginning a new 'unbinding' of potential in the initial breaking of bonds that have linked the macromolecules of raw food together. $DO_{192}$ of Air moves toward a higher potential by releasing the power (unbinding) of the atomic bond and entering the environment of possibilities inherent in the ionic state (making, literally, millions of new bondings possible). $DO_{48}$ of Impressions moves into the environment of electromagnetic fields at $RE_{24}$, the fixed ionic wave forms enabling a vast canvas of images. In each case the DO is partially 'taken apart', exposing an enormous arena of possibilities.

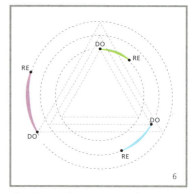

6

The RE – MI of all evolutionary octaves is a movement toward the appearance of the elementals of the particular food. For the raw Food Octave ($DO_{768}$) this is $MI_{19}$, the simplest of the amino acids, sugars and fats. They become the *building blocks* of the physical body.

Analogously, the $MI_{48}$ 'substances' of Air (the *neural, ionic wave forms*) are the *basic building blocks of the Kesdjan Body,* and the $MI_{12}$ 'substances' of Impressions (the remarkable attributes of the '*Attentions*' — the *'seeing' of what really is, by law*) are the *'building blocks' of the Higher Being-body.*

We approach the previous vague and seemingly absurd statements about the elementals of Kesdjan and Higher Being-body in this way:

△ The physical body, as previously noted, is made of thousands of complex and simple macromolecular substances. We are saying that the Kesdjan Body is made of complex and simple *images* that concern shared relationships between *self* and *other* (all *other*: people but also animals, plants and material 'things' like mountains, oceans, planets, etc.). Among other things, it is a direct perception of commonality, of what binds us together with, in the end, all created entities.

△ All of these images are essential (elemental) aspects of a completed Kesdjan Body and, like the elementals of the physical body, they will enter into many seemingly different combinations and sequences, as the laws of World 24 allow for exploration of the kaleidoscope of feeling (relational) images. To be kept in mind is that real 'feeling' includes a recognition and acceptance of commonality of being of the same Source, of shared values, and, as the Gurdjieff quotes emphasize, of 'seeings', of recognitions that can lead to the sacred impulse of Faith in the reality of the images as well as the feeling of the sacred impulse Love.

> "'And it is desirable because owing to faith alone does there appear in a being, the intensity of being-self-consciousness necessary for every being, and also the valuation of personal Being as of a particle of Everything Existing in the Universe.[16]

This is in marked contrast to the images created by the neural impulses that derive from $FA_{96}$ – the physical body processes. Here, opposites are imaged – the pleasant/unpleasant, like/dislike and yes/no of the automatic processes, which are dedicated to the maintenance and persistence of the physical body (via the first brain). There are *no* 'opposites' in the Kesdjanian images of $FA_{24}$ because they are always inclusive and acceptant of difference.

## Qualifications of the H12 Category

Before discussing specifically $MI_{12}$, the elementals of the Impressions Octave, the qualities and attributes of all $H12$ substances in three-brained beings will be outlined. Of premier importance is the **tripartite** nature of *Attention*; namely *focus*, *differentiation* and *creativity*.[17]

### $SI_{12}$ of Food—The 'Automatic' Attentions

Every level of our automatic functioning (under the Laws of World 48) includes an 'attention' which, however unconscious and 'mechanical', is the overall reconciling force (the energy 'exchange' particle) that *sees* and *affirms* the most appropriate resolution to the circumstance it is focused on. As the 'highest' energy ("Exioëhary" in Gurdjieff's terms), it is also the carrier of the reconciling force in the procreating of a new physical being and is also the 'force' behind the many manifestations of 'sex energy'. This $SI_{12}$ attention plays a vital role in all World 48 lawfulnesses (which are also energy manifestations of the first-brain survival triad). In the 'ordinary' life of World 48, with the survival triad of the first brain as the most potent determiner of manifestations, there is very limited freedom in the expression of the attentions. Many attentions operate well below the level of the waking consciousness (Gurdjieff's "second state of consciousness") and those that are available to the waking consciousness are not energetic enough to persist to a balanced conclusion. We have only to recall how easily our 'attention' is attracted or distracted by other impulses (from food, sex or survival) to confirm the limits of our 'attention-of-the-moment'. Even when we have sufficient attention to pursue an idea, a physical capacity or a feeling state, the result is not a full, three-brain integration of possible data. It is, rather, an example of Gurdjieff's "Reason-of-knowing."

---

16 Gurdjieff, *Beelzebub's Tales*, PP 191-192.
17 Buzzell, *see* the chapter, "Attention (H12), The Greatest Gift to Life; The Power to Pursue Meaning and Purpose," in *A New Conception of God, Further Reflections on Gurdjieff's Whim*; PP 280-99.

"And as for that Reason which for most of your contemporary favorites has become habitual and which I called the Reason-of-knowing, every kind of new impression perceived through this Reason, and likewise every kind of intentionally or simply automatically obtained result from formerly perceived impressions is only a temporary part of the being, and might result in them exclusively only in certain surrounding circumstances, and on the definite condition that the information which constitutes all his foundation and entirety should without fail be from time to time so to say 'freshened' or 'repeated'; otherwise these formerly perceived impressions change of themselves, or even entirely, so to say, 'evaporate' out of the common presence of the three-brained being.

"Although in respect of the Sacred Triamazikamno the process of the arising of both kinds of being-Reason flows equally, yet the fulfilling factors for the actualization of its three separate holy forces are different. ...."[18]

### SOL$_{12}$ *of Air—The Attentions of Higher Emotional Center*

The note SOL, of all evolutional octaves, marks the entry into the Harnel-Aoot, the disharmonized fifth Stopinder. It is here that the "clash" (the reconciliation) between the Holy-Affirming and Holy-Denying of the octave takes place. Being also of the 'hydrogen' 12 category of matter, it will express the three powers of attention (of *focus*, *differentiation* and *creativity*). And, finally, the quality of the state of consciousness will greatly alter the context and the possible results. This last sentence needs elaboration to try to make it clear. What we are saying is that Higher Centers are functional in three-brained beings even when they are 'half-asleep', in the second state of consciousness. While a three-brained being is not conscious of this Higher Center functioning, it continues to function throughout life and to have influence on the capacities and functional expression of all three-brained beings. There is great variability to this expression of Higher Center function. It may have no influence at all on the individual and hence there would not be even an unconscious expression of Higher Center function. In many people, however, there are a variety of manifestations, as all art, philosophy, spirituality and scientific enquiries are expressions of influence that ultimately derive from Higher Center functions. The major qualifier is that all of these expressions take place with the individual in the second state of consciousness. Thus, they are subjective expressions of an individual living under 48 orders of law—greatly affected by personality and egoism.

SOL is also an expression of the triad of the law of digestion or transformation[19] (2-1-3). The result of the digestive process at SOL depends largely on the intensity of the '1'–the middle force. If it is a high quality, the 3 (or result) will reflect this higher quality.

---

18 Gurdjieff, *Beelzebub's Tales*, PP 1166-67.
19 See illustration 21 in this volume, P 100.

The final qualification of $SOL_{12}$ is that it is the true entry into Higher Emotional Center. As Gurdjieff notes in *In Search*:

> "As has been said earlier, there are two higher centers:
> "The higher emotional center, working with hydrogen 12, and
> "The higher thinking center, working with hydrogen 6.[20]

How, then, can we understand the nature of $FA_{24}$ of the Air Octave? It lies after the first conscious shock but it is not yet of a high enough energy to proceed of itself into the true functional expression of Higher Emotional Center ($SOL_{12}$).

We have found it helpful to apply the analogy of the vestibule of a cathedral to the relationship of $FA_{24}$ to $SOL_{12}$. A vestibule is an entry point to the cathedral. While in the vestibule, there are hints about the magnificence and beauty that lies further on but there is also the recognition of the smallness, and 'ordinariness' of the vestibule. One recognizes that one is not in the cathedral itself, but at a necessary entry point. The 'pull' back into ordinary life is still very much present. This dual state of perception is the entry into the Harnel-Aoot, the lawful 2-1-3 (triad of transformation) and the *creative attention* of $SOL_{12}$ must act on and reconcile. This requires a great and continuing effort of Being, a true suffering 'between two stools', (the extraordinary creative potential of $SOL_{12}$ versus the restrictive conditional World 48 perspective).

The images created at $FA_{24}$ thus have a dual quality. They are real self-other images, but they contain much of personality, of unresolved conflicts, anxieties, etc.. The struggle to separate-from and eliminate the automatic and negative aspects of these self-other images is the entry into the Harnel-Aoot of $SOL_{12}$. One begins to step from the vestibule and have the first real glimpses of the interior of the cathedral.

### *Expressions of* $FA_{24}$ *toward* $SOL_{12}$

There is no denying the remarkable artistic expressions of individuals like J.S. Bach, Mozart, Picasso, Rembrandt, Botticelli, Michelangelo, Shakespeare, Pablo Casals, T.S. Eliot, and a great many other artists and performers. There are many capable musicians who are also poets, dancers and scientists. The manifestations of idiot savants, of Nobel prize-winning physicists who are also fine musicians, and of many of our acquaintances, who are drawn to express themselves in poetry, painting, music and pure scientific enquiry–they are all influenced by Higher Center (Emotional and Intellectual) function although they are not conscious of that function. It can be seen that the lack of consciousness (the third state of consciousness of Being) is what differentiates objective art from subjective art. Gurdjieff takes this difference up in considerable detail in the chapter "Art" of *The Tales*.

---

20 Ouspensky, *In Search*, p 194.

When the expression (artistic, emotional or scientific) is free of the personality, of egoism in its many forms, it then becomes more objective because it is 'outside' the personality (impartial to it) and present to the world of Being—sharing its expression outward into the world of *other*.

This expression may be one of:

~ beauty (in painting, poetry, music, dance, etc.),
~ common values, of Conscience-guided manifestation
   (of kindness, generosity, forgiveness),
~ insight into man's purposes (of community) and possibilities
   (in spiritual and philosophical scientific teaching).

All of these will have the Higher Emotional character of value and wish for *other*.

The degree of objectivity is determined by the degree of real presence in the third (and possibly touched by the fourth) state of consciousness. $SOL_{12}$ is the creative energy that is active within this broad arena of Being-capacities. Its expression is unique to the individual.

## $MI_{12}$ *of Impressions —The Attentions of Higher Intellectual Center*

The note MI of all evolutional octaves is the note where the elementals, the building blocks of the 'body' (which is to appear at FA), are formed. In the instance of the physical body, these are the amino acids, simple sugars and fats that will take form at $FA_{96}$ in the complex proteins and carbohydrate-fatty complexes of the structures of the physical body. With reference to the Air Octave, the elementals are the plethora of neural impulses that will be reformed into the images of the *self-other* world of the Kesdjan Body.

With respect to $MI_{12}$, the elementals of Higher Being-body are the creative insights, the glimpses of the form of Higher law, the entry point into Higher Reason and its crystallization. As a preparatory step toward Higher Being-body, it is also the 'stage' for creative experimentation—a setting-in-motion (a kind of 'testing'), a specific understanding of law (e.g., Gurdjieff's creating circumstances for Work for a particular group or individual and then evaluating the results).

At this level of the third state (and, potentially, of the fourth state) of consciousness ($SOL_{12}$ and $MI_{12}$), there is a blending of the efforts being made and the Higher Emotional and Higher Intellectual Center functions are often indistinguishable.

> ... emergent processes can be described by three principles: self-organization, novelty, and transcendence/inclusion. Familiarity with these concepts allows us to understand divine activity in a way consonant with the mystical insights of Christian tradition while honoring our deepest and most current perspectives of the natural sciences.[21]

---

21  Reho, James, "Liberating God from Heaven," (Parabola, Winter, 2013-2014), p 89.

# Food and Air Enneagrams

## Further Explorations in the Enneagrams of Physical Food and Air

When we look at the completed enneagram of physical Food (illustration 7), it is essential to keep in mind the long, evolutionary history that has been encapsulated in a prior segment.

As we have seen, the movement from $FA_{96}$ to $SOL_{48}$ (mass to non-mass), an event/process that is constantly taking place in each of us, took millions of years to develop in many incremental steps. How patient Great Nature is! Also to be reemphasized is that the entirety of the Food Octave takes place in the second state of consciousness.

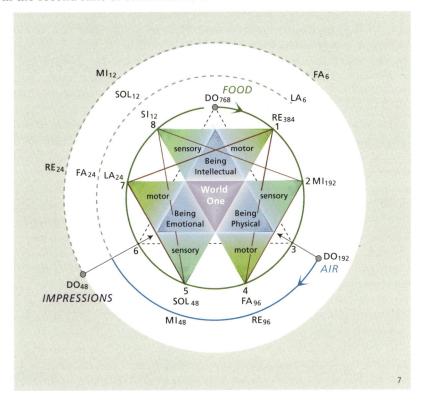

## $LA_{24}$ and $SI_{12}$ of the Food Octave

The completion of the octave of Food, in brained beings, is common to all reptilian, mammalian and human species and is the final realization ($SI_{12}$–DO) of the octave beginning from $DO_{768}$—namely in the reproduction of a macromolecular being. It takes place under the laws of World 48 and, thus, is entirely automatic. As noted by Gurdjieff, there is no conscious shock at $DO_{48}$, hence *no conscious continuation* of the Air or Impressions Octaves.

## *Automatic Results — What Precedes* $LA_{24}$

In neurophysiology, there is a principle known as the "All or None Law." This principle applies to all nerve cells in the body. Each nerve cell has many (sometimes thousands) of nerve fibers from other cells (dendrites) that carry either stimulatory or inhibitory impulses to the nerve cell. The nerve cell discharges (or initiates a nerve impulse in its axon) only when a certain threshold of electrical charge is reached and this is determined by the totality of the stimulatory and inhibitory impulses. If this threshold is reached, the nerve cell discharges totally ("all or none"). If the stimulatory input to the cell is below the threshold, then no discharge takes place.

What this means, in terms of the neural input that feeds vast quantities of data into the cortical associating centers, is that the image being created in the electromagnetic fields of the brain will reflect the same "all or none" quality–that sensation, feeling and thought images will reflect the 'yes/no', 'like/dislike', 'pleasant/unpleasant' of the all-or-none action of the nerve cells. The images produced in the moment will exclude the opposite sensation, feeling or thought that could derive from other sensory input. In that 'present moment' these opposites simply do not exist! *Our life of contradictions in the second state of consciousness derives from this.*

The neuronal input ($SOL_{48}$) is reporting on the state of affairs of the unique physical body, that which is the result of the half-father, half-mother DNA that directs the processes taking place at $FA_{96}$. The sensations, feelings and thoughts that result at $LA_{24}$ will reflect the individual quality of that experience. It is my pain, my like, my opinion–and it is not yours because my experience is unique, not shared. There are endless examples of this narrow and subjective experience in the second state of consciousness. I defend my uniqueness endlessly, saying, "You don't understand;" "My pain is deeper, worse than yours;" "My knowledge is deeper than yours therefore I am right." All this is automatic and, ultimately, derivative from the nature of the neuronal input from the unique physical body. Our subjective experience, while in the second state of consciousness, is also a result of the dominance of the survival triad of the first brain, where the focus is on the survival of my body and does not include *other*.

In one moment we are convinced, because of the automatically processed sensory input, that a particular sensation, feeling or thought is real and justifiable. A few moments later, we are equally convinced of the reality of the opposite sensation, feeling or thought. This is our situation in the second state of consciousness, living under 48 orders of law. Thus, we are caught in a dyadic world of perception. We are not conscious of just how contradictory to common sense this way of living actually is, because all of the ordinary people around us are living the same contradictory life! We do, occasionally, have moments when we see the absurdity of this situation, but it leads, at best, to frustration or to the momentary conviction that we will change and alter the biological, lawful process. Sadly, this conviction is another momentary 'yes/no' moment, evaporating very quickly.

## "Buffers" — or not?

Gurdjieff's presentations on "buffers" (in *In Search*, chapter 8) and Kundabuffer (in *Beelzebub's Tales*, throughout) are closely related to the 'yes/no' nature of the second state of consciousness. The *lack of* a simultaneous *yes and no* in our immediate experience points clearly to the fact that, while in a moment, we are conscious of one (yes), we are not, at the same time, conscious of the other (no). To be conscious of both, simultaneously, would be a different state of consciousness. In this view, Kundabuffer is *not a something*; rather it is the *absence of consciousness*. This is another way, perhaps, of pointing to the lack of a third force in our perception while in the second state of consciousness. It is a lawful 'automatic' circumstance under the laws of World 48 and would, thus, be a description applicable to one- and two-brained beings (as well as to three-brained beings while in the second state of consciousness).

## LA$_{24}$ of Physical Food

The images created at LA$_{24}$ of Food reflect the survival triad of the first brain. Sensory/motor images, having their underpinning processes at FA$_{96}$ and SOL$_{48}$, will reflect the present state of the physical body: its need (or not) for food, its defenses in moments of threat or conflict, the cyclic need for mating and reproduction and its vitality or weakness. Emotional images of the first brain are closely tied to the sensory/motor, with rage, suspicion, defensive and dominance displays (arrogance) predominant. Thinking images of the first brain are more difficult to speak about clearly, but it is known that if the very thin outer layer of the brain (that which evolves into the third brain or cerebral cortex) is removed or damaged, the creature remains inert, not 'moving out' into the surrounding world. This is a kind of commitment-into-action, an assessment and decisioning–out into life. It is also known that many one-brained creatures have clear memory of hunting grounds and show very clever planning and adaptive strategies in tracking prey. These could be considered the first-brain parallels to what we usually call "thinking."

Much human behavior reflects the triadic survival functions of the first brain. The majority of our world's suffering, aggression, arrogance, dominance and the lack of acceptance of difference is a direct expression of the continued, singular role played by the first brain. It also demonstrates the *limited* 'reality' of the second state of consciousness.

## SI$_{12}$ of Physical Food

We consider that the entirety of Gurdjieff's H12 category of matter concerns the *attentions* (the photonic powers: to focus–*creating* 1s, to differentiate–*creating* 2s, and to form patterns–*creating* 3s). In the physical Food Octave, SI$_{12}$ includes many levels of *attention*–all automatic (under 48 orders of law)–the highest of which Gurdjieff termed "Exioëhary," the energy that reconciles the egg and the sperm in sexual reproduction. There are many normal expressions of this sexual energy and Gurdjieff takes up, at considerable length, the *misuse* of this energy in the 'ordinary' life of brained beings.[22]

All attentions can be creative—if the third power of creating or making 3s is brought into action. For this, the attention has to be kept focused and a differentiation of the arena focused upon has to be maintained. Examples of this power abound in ordinary life, as all learning is a manifestation of this power and demonstrates that, to a certain degree, we can control or direct this attention, in particular when it concerns aspects of the external world (e.g., movements of physical bodies and being able 'to know' and predict movements in the outside world—Newton's Laws of Motion and Einstein's Relativity theories are of this order). Gurdjieff is referring to these powers of attention when he comments:

> "The two usual, that is, the lowest, states of consciousness are first, sleep, in other words a passive state in which man spends a third and very often a half of his life. And second, the state in which men spend the other part of their lives, in which they walk the streets, write books, talk on lofty subjects, take part in politics, kill one another, which they regard as active and call 'clear consciousness' or the 'waking state of consciousness.' The term 'clear consciousness' or 'waking state of consciousness' seems to have been given in jest, especially when you realize what clear consciousness ought in reality to be and what the state in which man lives and acts really is.[23]

## AIR—MI$_{48}$ of Air

The neural impulses created at MI$_{48}$ are ionic wave transformations of the processes taking place at RE$_{96}$ of Air. We have previously noted the quality of 'commonness' (of the air, hormones, enzymes, etc.,) that characterizes the Air Octave and this *shared quality* persists throughout the upper notes of the octave. Hence, MI$_{48}$ will 'report' on the state of vital, shared energies of motion and interaction/events which concern the being's interactions with other beings. Hormones, in particular, have formative and powerful roles to play in sexual expressions—including mating and reproduction—in expressions of contentment, pleasure, comfort, playfulness, connectedness, etc., (in varied groupings such as we see in mammalian life). All of these expressions are feelings that reflect *self-other* relationships. Lacking the first conscious shock, the individual creature is not conscious of them, but they are real expressions nonetheless.

## MI$_{48}$–FA$_{24}$ Interval of Air

At the MI$_{48}$–FA$_{24}$ interval, varied influences may enter that bring much unpredictability to the development of the octave. Gurdjieff's reference in

---

22 Ouspensky, *In Search*, p 257.
23 Ibid., p 141.

*In Search* (p 188) to the "element of emotion" that *may* enter with the first conscious shock is an example. We understand the "element of emotion" to be dependent on emotional influences that ultimately derive from Itoklanoz; early life experiences that are accessed via memory.

We come next to the entry into the third state of consciousness–at $FA_{24}$. Here it is useful to recall that the note FA of all evolutional octaves involves the transformation of the 'elementals' into the substance of the body, just as $FA_{96}$ of Food involves the creation of the proteins etc., that make up the form of the physical body. At $FA_{24}$, then, we are concerned with the substances that will form the Body of Kesdjan. And these substances are images.

How are these *images* different from those created at $LA_{24}$ of Food?

All images created at $FA_{24}$ concern both *self* and *other*. They are always images of 'me' *and* some aspect of the Universe. Most often, they are images that include other people–but they also include images of other life-forms (animals, plants) and other structures (oceans, lakes, rivers, mountains, weather phenomena, volcanoes, etc.,). Always the images are of a shared space, a participation in a shared event. It is never only me, my selfish, first-brain perspective. Because it incorporates the world around me in a relational way, it is a grand mix of images of feeling. It is not that these are necessarily pleasant or positive, only that they are more real because they include the Universe beyond myself. This is a truly three-dimensional perspective which includes the physical (sensory-motor), emotional and thinking functions. It may be confusing and upsetting–producing apprehension and unresolved issues or be warm and inviting of deeper relationship. It is unresolved but real and in need of further digestion at $SOL_{12}$ and $LA_6$, illustration 8, next page.

This is parallel to the $FA_{96}$ of the Food Octave. The substances making up the physical body do not determine the varied motions, efforts, skills and thinkings that an individual 'body' (person) may come to in its experiential life. Similarly, the images forming the substantiality of the Kesdjan Body do not determine the final capacities, insights, digested feelings and efforts of an individual.

## $SOL_{12}$ of Air

The *attentions* which are present and active at this point in the Air Octave have different qualities and attributes from those of $SI_{12}$. Some notion of this difference can be garnered from the enneagrammatic sequence of the Air Octave, illustration 8.

We have separated the representation of the Air Octave in order to highlight aspects of its inner circulation, note inner line rotation (in brown).

Note that on this illustration;

△ The interval 5 ($SOL_{12}$) – 7 ($LA_6$) is the Harnel-Aoot of this Octave. We associate this "disharmonized" interval with the Conscience-related transformation of negative emotions that must take place before the second conscious shock has its full influence.

# Third Striving

△ The presence of the second conscious shock takes place at the MI₁₂–FA₆ interval of Higher Being-body (the Impressions Octave). There is, thus, a simultaneity of sorts, with the final form of Kesdjan taking place with the appearance (at FA₆) of the elementally transformed functions and processes of Higher Being-body (in particular, in regard to Higher Reason).

△ The inner line 8 (SI₆) to 5 (SOL₁₂) brings the final aim of the individual's Kesdjanian existence, as an influence, into a firm focus. This always concerns a chosen *life of service*.

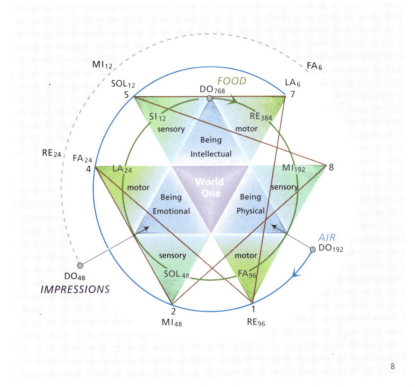

△ The inner line 5 (SOL₁₂)–7 (LA₆) aligns the attentions of Higher Emotional center to the aim of the coalescence of Real I. The inner movement from 5 (SOL₁₂)–7 (LA₆) is pointing toward the final 'form' or 'pattern' of the Kesdjan Body. This coalesced Body will have true, individual Will — a Real I.

The creative power of SOL₁₂ is its most notable aspect.[24] The highest power of SI₁₂ (Exioëhary or Attention) carries the reconciling force in the creation of a new life-form (of its physical body). The creative power of SOL₁₂ (a different quality of attention) concerns the self-creation of the Kesdjan Body. Also to have in mind is that SOL of all evolutional octaves is the entry

---

24 Buzzell, *see* the chapter "Attention (H12), The Greatest Gift to Life; The Power to Pursue Meaning and Purpose," in *A New Conception of God, Further Reflections on Gurdjieff's Whim*; pp 280-99.

into the disharmonized interval (the Harnel-Aoot). In other words, the outcome or final 'form' (at LA) is not guaranteed. Gurdjieff characterized this interval in this way:

> "As regards the third Stopinder, then changed in its 'subjective action' and which is fifth in the general successiveness and is called 'Harnel-Aoot,' its disharmony flowed by itself from the change of the two aforementioned Stopinders.
>
> "This disharmony in its subjective functioning, flowing from its asymmetry so to say in relation to the whole entire completing process of the sacred Heptaparaparshinokh, consists in the following:
>
> "If the completing process of this sacred law flows in conditions, where during its process there are many 'extraneously-caused-vibrations,' then all its functioning gives only external results.
>
> "But if this same process proceeds in absolute quiet without any external 'extraneously-caused-vibrations' whatsoever, then all the results of the action of its functioning remain within that concentration in which it completes its process, and for the outside, these results only become evident on direct and immediate contact with it.
>
> "And if, however, during its functioning there are neither of these two sharply opposite conditions, then the results of the action of its process usually divide themselves into the external and the internal.[25]

Our understanding, of this universal process, with respect to the Octave of Air and the 'role' of $SOL_{12}$, is this:

△ Every event in the life of a three-brained being can be understood as having an inner (subjective) and outer (objective) aspect. We each experience the inner world (subjective) of sensations, feelings and thoughts in each of life's events. On the objective (or outer) side, there are those actions – the words spoken, the gestures and motions (the 'doings'). These are, lawfully, infused by and reflect the inner world.

△ If the event of the moment is one of a deep, meditative effort, then the flow or 'process' through the Harnel-Aoot (the SOL–LA) is almost exclusively subjective (inner) and the "results of the action of its functioning remain within that concentration in which it completes its process and for the outside these results only become evident on direct and immediate contact with it" ("becoming evident" when outer world contact with *other* is made). If one remains quiet, all of the "results" remain within his inner, subjective world.

△ If the event is an intense and relational one, with the emphasis on outer manifestation, then "all its functioning gives only external results." The *doing*, the external act of kindness, compassion, etc., brings about a change in the external world of manifestation. However, as Gurdjieff qualifies this

---

25 Gurdjieff, *Beelzebub's Tales*, pp 754-55.

process, "the results of the action usually divide themselves into the external and the internal." The external action is what it is (outer) but something takes place in the inner world (e.g., a deepening of understanding the law, and increase in the feeling of compassion).

The creative power of $SOL_{12}$ is evident here. Each event of life presents a circumstance. Always there is the question: "What is the most appropriate feeling, thought and external manifestation in this particular situation?" Here, the degree of understanding the laws (the degree of Reason) has to be applied. At the same time, there is the 'circumstance' of the most helpful 'feeling' to be expressed with Conscience at its core. Choices have to be explored and made – and this is the test of the creativity of $SOL_{12}$.

Irmis Popoff, our early Work mentor, was known by all her students for her ability to create circumstances, within whatever the event was, that made Work-in-the-moment a reality. We could be preparing food, painting a wall, feeding the cats or engaged in conversation–and she would suddenly present us with a demand–or a question–which would bring us to attention, to an effort to be present or to see the workings of the law. It was said that Ouspensky, her early mentor, once told her, with emphasis, "Irmis, you are always inventing." Initially, she understood this as a criticism, but in time, she began to see this as a creative opportunity, a gift–a moment in which she could create circumstances that could be of immense value to our personal and collective Work. We understand her 'creativity' in those moments as having the simultaneous 'inside/outside' quality that Gurdjieff is referring to in the quotation. Life is full of these opportunities to apply our Reason and emotional understanding to the relational task at hand. When we do, we are making effort to stand in this $SOL_{12}$–$LA_6$ interval of Air, *within* ourselves.

## INFLUENCES OF THE FIRST CONSCIOUS SHOCK

We must look carefully at the placement of the first conscious shock in the three octaves. It is placed not only at the DO of the Impressions Octave but is a potent influence on the $SOL_{48}$–$LA_{24}$ of the Food Octave and on the $MI_{48}$–$FA_{24}$ of the Air Octave (see illustration, P 37). Thus, there are three distinct processes taking place. The differentiation of these processes has not always been made clear (to our awareness) in Work literature. In *In Search* (117-18) the first steps in this differentiation are clearly set down:

> "Not one of you has noticed the most important thing that I have pointed out to you," he said. "That is to say, not one of you has noticed that you do not remember yourselves." (He gave particular emphasis to these words.) "You do not feel yourselves; you are not conscious of yourselves. With you, 'it observes' just as 'it speaks' 'it thinks,' 'it laughs.' You do not feel: I observe, I notice, I see. Everything still 'is noticed,' 'is seen.' ... In order really to observe oneself one must first of all remember oneself" (He again emphasized these words.) "Try to

remember yourselves when you observe yourselves and later on tell me the results. Only those results will have any value that are accompanied by self-remembering. Otherwise you yourselves do not exist in your observations. In which case what are all your observations worth?"

These words of G.'s made me think a great deal. It seemed to me at once that they were the key to what he had said before about consciousness. But I decided to draw no conclusions whatever, but to try to remember myself while observing myself.

The very first attempts showed me how difficult it was. Attempts at self-remembering failed to give any results except to show me that in actual fact we never remember ourselves.

"What else do you want?" said G. "This is a very important realization. People who know this" (he emphasized these words) "already know a great deal. The whole trouble is that nobody knows it. If you ask a man whether he can remember himself, he will of course answer that he can. If you tell him that he cannot remember himself, he will either be angry with you, or he will think you an utter fool. The whole of life is based on this, the whole of human existence, the whole of human blindness. If a man really knows that he cannot remember himself, he is already near to the understanding of his being."

All that G. said, all that I myself thought, and especially all that my attempts at self-remembering had shown me, very soon convinced me that I was faced with an entirely new problem which science and philosophy had not, so far, come across.

There is another qualification, *(ISM, p 188)*

"There is, however, a possibility of increasing the output, that is, of enabling the air octave and the impression octave to develop further. For this purpose it is necessary to create a special kind of 'artificial shock' at the point where the beginning of the third octave is arrested. This means that the 'artificial shock' must be applied to the note do 48.

"But what is meant by an 'artificial shock'? It is connected with the moment of the reception of an impression. The note do 48 designates the moment when an impression enters our consciousness. An 'artificial shock' at this point means a certain kind of effort made at the moment of receiving an impression.

"It has been explained before that in ordinary conditions of life we do not remember ourselves; we do not remember, that is, we do not feel ourselves, are not aware of ourselves at the moment of a perception, of an emotion, of a thought or of an action. If a man understands this and tries to remember himself, every impression he receives while remembering himself will, so to speak, be doubled. In an ordinary psychic state I simply look at a street. But if I remember myself, I do not simply look at the street; I feel that I am looking, as though saying to myself: 'I am looking.' Instead of one impression of the street there are two impressions, one of the street and another of myself looking at it. This second impression, produced by the fact of my remembering myself, is the 'additional shock.' Moreover, it very often happens that the additional sensation connected with self-remembering brings with it an element of emotion, that is, the work of the machine attracts a certain amount of 'carbon' 12 to the place in question. Efforts to remember oneself, observation of oneself at the moment of receiving an impression, observation of one's impressions at the moment of receiving them, registering, so to speak, the reception of impressions and the simultaneous defining of the impressions received, all this taken together doubles the intensity of the impressions and carries do 48 to re 24. At the same time the effort connected with the transition of one note to another and the passage of 48 itself to 24 enables do 48 of the third octave to come into contact with mi 48 of the second octave and to give this note the requisite amount of energy necessary for the transition of mi to fa. In this way the 'shock' given to do 48 extends also to mi 48 and enables the second octave to develop.

"Mi 48 passes to fa 24; fa 24 passes to sol 12; sol 12 passes to la 6. La 6 is the highest matter produced by the organism from air, that is, from the second kind of food. This however is obtained only by making a conscious effort at the moment an impression is received.

Note the following:

△ How, exactly, is one to understand the expression "to *re*-member oneself?" Seen from one perspective, it could be understood to mean "to put the 'self' back together from its presently dismembered state." This way of looking at the expression implies that at some point in the past one's self was not dismembered. Or, does the expression "self-remembering" also (or instead of) carry an emphasis on memory and, if so, remembering of what? our body?

△ In the first quotation, Gurdjieff emphasizes that "in order really to observe oneself one must first of all remember oneself." Clearly these are two distinct efforts, with self-remembering preceding self-observation. If self-remembering is not present, then the result is the observation of one center by another center. This is the essence of 'talking to oneself'—a common psychic process that all of us can readily identify. At other times, Gurdjieff emphasized that efforts to self-remember must be made over a considerable time (perhaps years) before one can properly self-observe.

△ An essential point here is that self-remembering and self-observation are different psychic processes and Gurdjieff associates both of them with the first conscious shock. "Otherwise you yourselves do not exist in your observations." To establish our Being, a presence to your physical existence in this moment, is fundamental to the state of self-remembering. The primary emphasis placed by Gurdjieff on sensing the body (in parts, or whole, in sequence or in toto) is intimately related to establishing that presence. The practice of sensing is itself a complex, multilayered and subtle endeavor, one which requires increasing sensitivity to processes taking place within and beyond the body. Over time, successive 'layers' are revealed and the structures (skin, flesh, muscle, organs) and the energies associated with each become delineated. The 'Being', one's existence-in-the-moment, becomes more broadly established in both form and process.

△ Note in the second quotation, the sentences "In an ordinary psychic state I simply look at a street. But if I remember myself, I do not simply look at the street; I feel that I am looking, as though saying to myself: 'I am looking.' Instead of one impression of the street there are two impressions, one of the street and another of myself looking at it." Clearly this points to an *awareness* of the processes taking place at $LA_{24}$ of the Food Octave. All of the sensory data (outer and inner) that results in the images of $LA_{24}$ is available to be seen ("I feel that I am looking"). In this comment, Gurdjieff is pointing to a division. The second state of consciousness (a consciousness common also to one- and two-brained beings) *does not* include a separated awareness-of-being-aware. That separated state of awareness shows itself with the effort to self-remember at $DO_{48}$. This division of the attention is the basis of self-observation, the 'seeing' of the automatic and negative images that appear at $LA_{24}$ of the Food Octave from an *impartial perspective*.

In the second state of consciousness, neither animal (one-/two-brained) or man can 'see' the actions, feelings or thoughts from an inner separated perspective. One is wholly identified with these images — becoming them in the sense that the acting, feeling or thinking self-of-the-moment says 'I' ("I see the book; I feel sad; I think I know") to each of them.

△ The second state of consciousness is a 'result' of the neural processes that derive from the monitoring of bodily functions. The energies (the 'hydrogen' materialities) for this are produced by the digestion of food and are wholly dedicated to the survival of the physical body (resulting in the survival triad of the first brain). The images created at $LA_{24}$ of the Food Octave, therefore, will reflect the automaticities and negativities that derive from this focus on the survival of the physical body. Gurdjieff's focus on survival in the moment (the underpinning of war), food and sexuality (the three poles of the survival triad) gives emphasis to the importance of the impartial observation that results from the $DO_{48}$–$RE_{24}$ of the Impressions Octave.

△ In the second quotation (p 46, line 4), starting with "Moreover, it very often happens...", there is a clear inference that:
1) it does not always happen, and
2) the "element of emotion" appears to come from the past of the individual, in the influences that derive from Itoklanoz.

We quote here from Gurdjieff's description of Itoklanoz, as these influences play essential roles in delineating the 'element of emotion' that may enter with the attention at the point of the incoming impression:

(1) Heredity in general

(2) Conditions and environment at the moment of conception

(3) The combination of the radiations of all the planets of their solar system during their formation in the womb of their productress

(4) The degree of being-manifestation of their producers during the period they are attaining the age of responsible being

(5) The quality of being-existence similar to themselves around them

(6) The quality of what are called the 'Teleokrimalnichnian' thought-waves formed in the atmosphere surrounding them also during their period of attaining the age of majority—that is, the sincerely manifested good wishes and actions on the part of what are called the 'beings-of-the-same-blood,' and finally,

(7) The quality of what are called the being egoplastikoori of the given being himself, that is his being-efforts for the transubstantiation in himself of all the data for obtaining objective Reason.[26]

From (4) through (7), the "good customs and 'automatic habits'" enter the individual and, with the movement of the attention to the point of incoming impressions, they bring the element of emotion required to assist the Air Octave to pass the $MI_{48}$–$FA_{24}$ interval.

The images of right behavior, of respectful relationship and of exposure to the natural and created beauties of the world are influences derived from (4) to (6) and enter via the memory of the individual.

In contrast to the above, we point to the description of the upbringing of Lentrohamsanin,[27] a process which provided nothing positive for the inner world of Lentrohamsanin. There were no positive qualities of emotion that could enter with the attention—and hence the Air Octave proceeded no further than $MI_{48}$ in him. It is important to note that Lentrohamsanin had no Being, (no development of the Air Octave) largely because the process of his Itoklanoz was totally bereft of any positive values or emphasis on right behavior.

△ Sensing the body was noted earlier as an essential aspect of the establishment of Being; a focus of the attention on the physical beingness of the body. This is bringing the third state of consciousness to the $LA_{24}$ of the Food Octave—penetrating into the second state of consciousness. The practice of following or being present to the breath brings a higher consciousness to the instinctive act of breathing (the earlier steps, the $DO_{192}$–$RE_{96}$–$MI_{48}$ of the Air Octave). The effort to be conscious of the breath brings an added positive influence to the $MI_{48}$–$FA_{24}$ interval of Air, assisting the "emotion" which often accompanies the attention (as Gurdjieff noted).

---

26 Gurdjieff, *Beelzebub's Tales*, pp 438-39.
27 Ibid., pp 392-95.

## In Sum

There are three distinct results that are coincident in the first conscious shock.

△ A higher consciousness is brought into the automaticities and negativities that result from the processes involved in the second state of consciousness (the physical Food Octave). Over time, this enables the impartial observation of our movements, feelings and thoughts.

△ A higher consciousness is brought to the $MI_{48}$–$FA_{24}$ interval of the Air Octave. Here, the attention penetrates into the images of the feeling (emotional) life, making possible the conscious juxtaposition of images of higher values, of right relationship, of beauty in sound and form together with the images that derive from the automatic and egoistic life of World 48 (of body and survival as perceived in the second state of consciousness). This juxtaposition is the entry point into the long struggle toward Conscience, filled with 'suffering' (the clash between the automaticities of our lower nature and the aspirations toward our higher nature). Bringing attention to the breath energizes the entirety of the Air Octave and greatly increases the extraction of the higher 'hydrogens' from the air (e.g., the digestion of images in sounds and pheromones within the air).

We are not referring here to breathing exercises – varying the rhythm, depth or speed of respiration or enforcing some pattern on breathing. We are referring only to the bringing of the attention to our normal respirations, including those changes of rate and depth that result from normal bodily functions (e.g., walking, running, practice of movements).

△ Quite distinct from the above mentioned results is the establishment of a separate and impartial presence. This is the true $DO_{48}$ of the Impressions Octave itself–establishing the possibility (much further on in this octave) of a singular I; an I with true Will. This is not the same as the establishment of Being (a prolonged effort that concerns primarily the feeling [Air Octave] and physical [Food Octave]–Worlds). Here, reference to the dilemma faced by the Toof-Nef-Tef (*BT*, pp 1148-51) may be helpful to clarify this. Having real Being and Conscience, the Toof-Nef-Tef lacks only Higher Reason– and this attainment requires an even higher development of the Impressions Octave (beyond the second conscious shock).

This consideration is a difficult one to speak about specifically, as the Higher Emotional (feeling) and Higher Intellectual (thinking) centers blend their functional expression at the level of 'hydrogen' 12 ($SOL_{12}$ and $MI_{12}$). Nonetheless, it is necessary to see that a fundamental understanding of Law (both cosmic and local) reaches beyond even the attainment of real Conscience. The ultimate answers to our "why" and "how" questions lie at this highest level of the Impressions Octave. The onset of this journey lies with the first conscious shock.

### $DO_{48}$–$RE_{24}$–$MI_{12}$ OF THE FOOD OF IMPRESSIONS ENNEAGRAM

We understand the Impressions Octave as concerning the inwardly 'separated' and impartial presence, in pursuit of a deeper comprehension of the Laws of Worlds 24, 48 and 96 (an encapsulation of the Third Striving). The initiation of this effort must come from World 12, the origin of the Lateral Octave. This is an attribute of the fourth state of consciousness, able to see and come to deep understanding of the triads of law that obtain in the life of the Earth. That deep understanding includes the worlds of practical manifestation of the body and true emotion. It is a lifelong journey for a three-brained being to create the 'elementals' (the MI) of three-centered Reason that will form the Higher Being-body.

It is our view that the Food Octave ($DO_{768}$—$SI_{12}$) nourishes and makes possible the varied 'motions' possible for a physical body. Its sensory/motor, feeling and thinking are commensurate with that level of forms and energies. It is, fundamentally, the carrier of the Holy-Denying force in the triad of all life. The first brain is its center-of-gravity functioning.

The Air Octave ($DO_{192}$—$SI_6$) nourishes and makes possible the varied expressions and understandings of the feeling (Kesdjan) Body. It is invested within the physical body, influencing, in the end, every cell with the direct perception of *self* and *other* in right relationship. It radiates beyond into the planetary world. The unearthing of our deeply buried Conscience is the primary pursuit in the upper notes of the Air Octave. It is, fundamentally, the carrier of the Holy-Reconciling force in the triad of all life. The second brain is its center-of-gravity functioning.

The Impressions Octave ($DO_{48}$ — $FA_6$–$SOL_6$–$LA_6$–$SI_6$–Higher Degrees of Reason) nourishes and makes possible the intellectual, feeling and practical understanding of the laws of Worlds 24, 48 and 96 (illustration 9 on the next page). It is also invested within the physical body but reaches beyond into the photonic world of the solar system. It is, fundamentally, the carrier of the Holy-Affirming force in the triad of all life. The third brain (Neocortex or Higher Intellectual Center) is its center-of-gravity functioning.

The initial aim, in sounding the $DO_{48}$ of Impressions, is the establishment of a 'separated' inner presence; a firm awareness of Being, which is within but not of the physical or feeling perceptual processes. Gurdjieff referred to this effort, or state, in a number of expressions, the most common being "self-remembering."

From this inner separated state (which is the entry point of the fourth state of consciousness), it is possible to see, to observe the automatic functioning of the physical body and its functional expressions in bodily sensory/motor, feelings and thinkings (the "formatory apparatus" of Gurdjieff). Over time, the working out of the laws (of World 48) becomes more apparent and the individual actively commits to participation in life's events but with an impartial presence. This commitment, into the observation and study of everyday life from an impartial, separated presence, is the note $RE_{24}$. The images created here are impartial representations of automatic processes the six primary laws,[36] which obtain in that particular level of life (i.e., Microcosmos > Tetartocosmos > brained life). We suggest the reader to refer to all illustrations, as they exhibit different aspects that are being addressed.

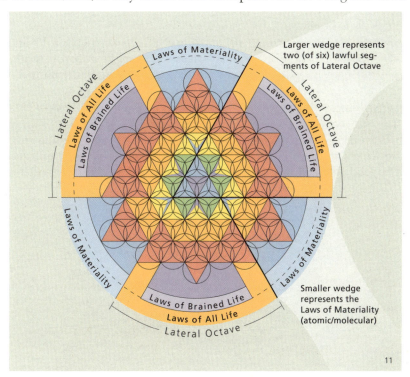

△ It is at the level of World 24 (orange triads) that the pattern of life is established. This is a truly miraculous, creative achievement! From it emerges the first life–the microcosmic world of single-celled life–the bacteria and earliest of single-celled organisms. This is the la of the Lateral Octave–the arising of the "Similitudes-of-the-Whole."

△ We have discussed the deflection of the Law of Three from the Law of Seven (Ilnosoparno). This 'deflection' makes possible the *persistence* (the Being—Law of Three) of chemical and whole life-forms, while *change* (the Becoming—Law of Seven) is interwoven such that–death and reproduction become reconcilers of these two great lawful expressions.[37]

△ It is notable that the Lateral Octave is constructed of three overlapping triads (each with triads from Worlds One, Three, Six, 12, 24 and 48). The triads of World 12, 24 and 48 that form the apices of the large overall triad of *A Symbol* (filled with blue, illustration 11, named "Laws of Materiality")

---

36 See illus. 21 on p 100 in this volume, and Buzzell, *A New Conception of God*, p 262.
37 In considering the meaning of the forms of life that emerge on *A Symbol*, refer to the discussion of the "Sacred Impulses: Faith, Hope and Love," chapter 7 in *Explorations in Active Mentation* (Salt Lake City: Fifth Press, 2006).

# Third Striving

represent laws that concern energies (high gamma, X-rays, ultraviolet) that are essential to the universal creative process but are of such high energies as would tear apart (unbond) atomic-molecular life.

## Apices of Triads

△ On *A Symbol* (illustration 12, detail) we have placed a large black dot at the confluence of one of the apices of six triads which are identified as triads of law for the note si (pattern of life), la (Microcosmos), sol (Tetartocosmos), fa (one-brained), sol (two-brained) and la (three-brained). This apex identifies the essentiality of the physical body.

△ The confluence marked with the black square lies at the outer apex of a World Six triad (green—recall that there are six of these apices in the enneagram we make use of in the World Six form). We consider this apex to be the Highest Intellect, which plays a role in do and si of the Lateral Octave, three-brained beings, Kesdjan and Higher Being-body.

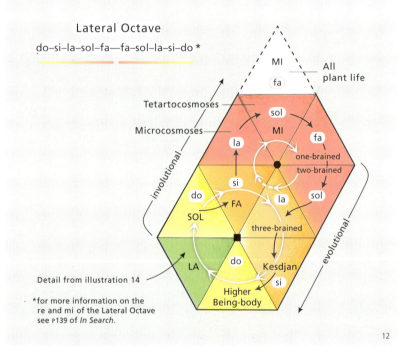

12

△ Notable is that the Kesdjan Body and the Higher Being-body do not share an apex with the shared apex of the physical body. Their bodies are of a different materiality.

△ Notable also is that the do (Will) – si (pattern of life) – la (Microcosmoses) – sol (Tetartocosmoses) – fa (plants) is an involutional motion, whereas the fa (one-brained), sol (two-brained), la (three-brained), si (Kesdjan Body) and do (Higher Being-body) is an evolutional motion.

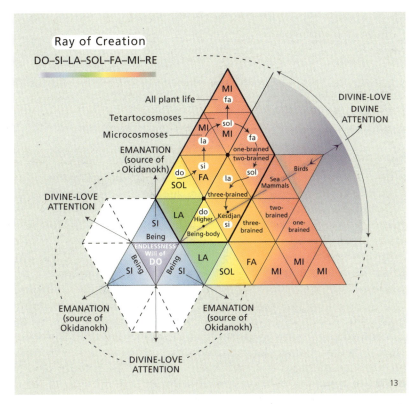

△ The center violet line, with arrows (illustration 13) which is identified as "Divine Attention—Divine-Love," passes through the center points and an apex of birds, sea mammals, Kesdjan and Higher Being-body and with one apex of two-brained and three-brained life. This line and the apices concern the feeling (emotional) impulse entering each brained form.

△ The triad of all plant life (fa of the Lateral Octave) unfolds from Tetartocosmos (sol), as does the triad of one-brained life (fa). The one-brained life triad unfolds from Tetartocosmos over the line which defines all brained life as lying within the Divine Attention and Divine-Love. This simultaneity, of two *fas* unfolding, represents the great division between photosynthetic organisms (plants) that digest $CO_2$ and excrete $O_2$ and brained organisms who digest $O_2$ and excrete $CO_2$. A great balance is, thus, maintained in the atmosphere of Earth.

△   △   △

## Times

*A Symbol of the Cosmos and Its Laws* is a static representation that obviously cannot properly reflect the temporal sequence of events. It is important to emphasize this fact as *A Symbol* reflects a present view of a creative process that has been in motion for some 14 billion years. The effort to sense, feel and think of processes that progress over such incredible lengths of time brings us up against an insurmountable barrier; the perceptions of process that derive from our physical body. Our average time on Earth, somewhere around 80 years, is less than a fraction of a fraction of a second in the life of our Sun (estimated to be 8-9 billion years). The duration of our Universe adds another 5 to 6 billion years. The Lateral Octave, to which we belong, is approximately 4.5 million years in duration, placing our lifetimes in a context wherein our individual lives appear to be inconsequential.

And yet, at the present, we are aware of this nearly unbelievable process of the unfolding of the Universe. We have a multitude of questions about this circumstance and beliefs abound concerning the significance of our individual and collective lives, of our 'place' in the life of the Universe.

One of the obvious facts about the history of mankind on Earth is that we, as a race of three-brained beings, have learned a great deal about the physical world. When I try to place myself in the circumstance of my forebears of ten thousand years ago, I am impressed by the practical knowledge they possessed concerning how to stay alive. They knew a good deal about the edible plants, the patterns of the animals they hunted, the clothing they made, the dwellings they constructed. They also had begun to domesticate animals and to plant crops. They were clearly relational beings, living in family and related groups. Historians trace the arising and spreading of these groups, eventually forming larger communities and early cities. From these, even larger groupings arose, largely mono-ethnic in type, with the city-state and warfare appearing. History, as reported by most, is a history of the rise of master/slave cultures and of large-scale conflicts between them. This is a recounting of mankind in the second state of consciousness, living under 48 orders of law.

*There is another history*, one that is not as well known but that demonstrates a very different perspective on mankind's role on the Earth. Joseph Campbell, through his many books[38] is, perhaps, the finest modern exemplar of this creative-mythologic perspective.

His books trace a long line of traditions, extending into prehistoric times and discussing higher powers, gods, man's higher purpose and possibilities, and the methodologies that were made use of to make contact with these higher states. His books incorporate oriental as well as occidental viewpoints and, while many of these are fanciful and full of imaginary beings and circumstances, they highlight the notion that there is far more (and hidden) than the drudgery, physical suffering and egoism so evident in many ancient cultures. The purpose of man's life lay beyond the physical reality, in worlds where different laws obtain and different fates exist.

In these two perspectives (the physical-historical and the mythological), we find echoes of the state of affairs that Gurdjieff described in his mythological treatment of Atlantis (in *Beelzebub's Tales*). There is the standard

---

38  Campbell, Joseph, *The Masks of God*, 4 volumes, (Penguin Arkana, 1991) *The Hero with the Thousand Faces*. (Novato: New World Library, 2008).

historical situation of a society that requires rigid adherence to certain codes (e.g., paying taxes) in order to remain stable. At the same time, there are individuals like Belcultassi and a society (the Akhaldans) that is in pursuit of the reality of their inner world which is fundamentally based on the striving toward Conscience and the onset of the pursuit of Objective Reason. The result is a culture under 48 orders of law, which is perceived from the second state of consciousness – *and* an 'interior' grouping of individuals who were simultaneously in contact with their inner world and were dedicated to entirely different aims than the general society. We can rightly infer that they were in pursuit of higher states of consciousness (living under 24 or even 12 orders of law).

From the scenario created by Gurdjieff, we can generalize to all societal groupings from ancient to modern. There will always be a larger, physically dominant population living under 48 orders of law. And there will always be a smaller population who seek for meaning and purpose, finding a broader 'reality' with greater potential in the inner world of man. This grouping, according to Gurdjieff, is not isolated from the larger group, but coexists with them – carrying on their responsibilities in ordinary life but always, and simultaneously, in pursuit of greater understanding and a higher level of Being.

This is true throughout the history of all civilizations. In nearly all large-scale historical events in human history, it is possible to identify a focal effort, most often associated with an individual and which, appropriate to the time, focused on the inner world of man and his responsibilities and possibilities. Such figures as Lao Tzu, the Hindu masters, Moses, Christ, Mohammed, the Buddha and the Tibetan Lamas – all were, in Gurdjieff's terms, "Messengers sent from Above" and each carried an impulse that resulted in an exterior, World 48 form and, simultaneously, an inner, World 24 form which spoke to mankind of a world far different than the historical master/slave, warfare thrust of the current civilization.

## Contemporary Times

In the Western world, there does not appear to be a singular thrust of this type since the time of Mohammed. While the intervening 1,400 years show evidences of 'inner renewals' (e.g., in certain aspects of the Christian monastic tradition and in the alchemical teachings of the Middle Ages), no singular Messenger appears who is responsible for a civilization-wide movement. If anything, we find a progressive condensation of belief systems adhering to the World 48 second state of consciousness and, with the rise of Western scientific disciplines, a concentration on the nature of the outer world of bodies and the energies that motivate these bodies. The inner world of feeling, of interpersonal relationships, has became grossly neglected, becoming Gurdjieff's little planet Anulios whose name even grandmothers have forgotten in their telling of fairy tales.[39]

---

39  Gurdjieff, *Beelzebub's Tales*, p 85.

## Third Striving

By the latter 19th century, the tension between city-states of Western civilization was approaching a world war status and the rise of Western science (including, majorly, the works of Darwin) and the quantum revolution was approaching a critical interface.

Looking back at this historical period, one can sense and perceive the critical juncture that was being approached by this civilization. The inner world of man had been progressively shredded to insignificance and warfare threatened the entirety of mankind. An effort to avert a worldwide catastrophe had to be made – from within the "Akhaldans" throughout the world. This is how we understand the many diverse efforts that entered the Western world, primarily but not exclusively, from the East. Here, we point to the influx of 'teachers' from the Hindu and Buddhist traditions and a number of Christian, Hebrew and Islamic (Sufi) scholars and teachers who gained influence from the early days of the 20th century to the present. Premier, among these carriers of the Holy-Reconciling force, was G. I. Gurdjieff. Emerging from a crossroad of the East and the West, he represents, among many other aspects, a blending of the scientific disciplines of the West (its focus on materialities and process) with the wisdom (the understandings and methods) of the East. One can find many resonances with the teachings of Christianity, Sufism, Buddhism, the Hebrew tradition and Lamaism but there is a singularity to Gurdjieff's teaching in his simultaneous encompassing of modern science and teachings of all of the Great Messengers regarding the inner world of man. In a very real sense, Gurdjieff is a Messenger but one who has *arisen from below*, blending the ancient mystic teaching of the inner world with the thoroughly modern world of the scientific disciplines.

The conflict within and between present day civilizations is ongoing and unresolved. We continue to approach a possible catastrophe on a global scale – witness our ecological disasters, the environmental degradation, the population explosion of humans, the warming climate, endangerment to or extinction of many species of animals and the ever-present state of warfare.

The need for an expanding and constant effort to bring mankind to a greater awareness of its inner world and outer world (the primary thrust of the Third Striving) has been evident since the latter 19th century. The stark reality in today's world is one that emphasizes the precariousness of the entire Lateral Octave of life on Earth. With all of science's technological 'progress' we are, as a worldwide society, now standing on the edge of a precipice, trapped in the second state of consciousness and, so far, unable to commit ourselves broadly to a real reconciliation of our inner and outer worlds. This is a challenge that is faced by all reflections of 'Work', whether it is clothed in restatements of, and external-life demonstrations of the Great Traditions, such as we see in the life of figures like Krishnamurti, Desmond Tutu, HH Dalai Lama, Dag Hammarskjöld and Martin Luther King but including the lesser known but increasingly essential demonstrations of compassion, kindness and acceptance manifested in thousands of daily events by many thousands of people who are awakening to the reality of the responsibilities and possibilities of a consciousness of the inner world. The most inclusive and comprehensive of these efforts, for us, is the system introduced by Gurdjieff – because he includes, not only the core of Conscience-aligned effort but also, the understanding and utilization of the energies of both outer and inner worlds (Worlds 48 and 24), the worlds that are the focus of modern scientific endeavors, and the plethora of practical, 'physical' manifestations of the body that demonstrate a balance between the sensory/motor, feeling and thinking aspects of a three-brained being.

A number of these efforts being made by modern representatives of the Great Traditions include aspects of the three efforts just noted, but the Gurdjieff teaching is balanced, inclusive and appropriate for our time.

## THE LATERAL OCTAVE AND THE CYCLE OF LIFE

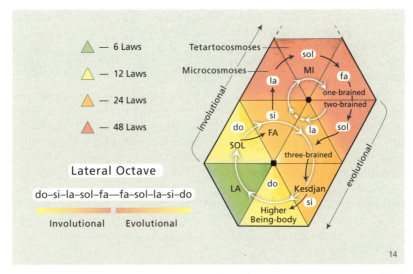

There are a number of resonances between the previous segments and inferences, drawn from the form of the Lateral Octave, which we will continue to explore on a detail of *A Symbol of the Cosmos and Its Laws*, (illustration 14).

The first of these concerns our individual appearance as three-brained beings in the Lateral Octave. In the illustration, there are two white circles to which we call attention. The smaller of the circles joins six triads (the si of the Lateral Octave; la > Microcosmos; sol > Tetartocosmos; fa > one-brained; sol > two-brained; and la > three-brained). The direction of the dark gray arrows is determined by the enneagrammatic pattern within the initial si.

Each of us, embryologically, follows this circle. The enneagrammatic pattern of life is established at the si. We are each conceived as a Microcosmos (a one-celled being) at la. We then grow to be a Tetartocosmos (a multi-celled being) at sol. When the central nervous system begins to develop, we are, initially, one-brained (fa), then two-brained (sol) and, finally, three-brained (la). We live out our life, hopefully, as a true three-brained being. We say hopefully because, although the natural home (by law) of a three-brained being is to live under 24 orders of Law, we often live much of our life as a two-brained, or even a one-brained being. Living the life of a true three-brained being is already a 'big' thing, because the triad of a three-brained being is a law of World 24 (note its orange color compared to the red color of a two-brained or one-brained being).

If one lives one's life as a three-brained being without having created a Kesdjan Body, the cycle would appear to come to an end. Our physical body dies—and Gurdjieff is very non-committal in talking specifically about the 'life force' that energizes this physical body. J.G. Bennett put forward a perspective on this question that is resonant with a completion of this circle (note the dashed line joining the triad of a three-brained being [la] with the si of the Lateral Octave). Bennett spoke of the "soul stuff pool" as a way of pointing to a 'recycling' of sorts that takes place at the death of the physical body. This white dashed line (si/three-brained) is also commensurate with Ouspensky's notion of "recurrence" although he emphasized the continuance of the same life. Various doctrines of reincarnation are also commensurate with the inference of this dotted line. Withal, it is an interesting inference of possible significance drawn from the form of the Lateral Octave.

The larger circle (with the square at its center) includes LA and SOL of the Great Ray, the si of the Lateral Octave, and the la (three-brained), si (Kesdjan) and do (Higher Being-body). The shared apices (the square) joins Cosmic Laws (LA and SOL of the Great Ray) with the si of the Lateral Octave, la (three-brained), si (Kesdjan) and do (Higher Being-body), inferring a shared level of understanding of Cosmic Law in all of these triads. Also, it could be inferred that the Higher Intellectual Center of three-brained beings *does* have access to the understanding of high Cosmic Law, as would certainly be true for Kesdjan and Higher Being-body. There are six of these shared apices in the enneagram of three-brained beings.

### From Three-brained to Kesdjan

Every three-brained being moves through the 'circle of life' in the Lateral Octave. A small number of three-brained beings will complete the creation of a Kesdjanian Body and the triad of his/her three-brained nature will fold over two apices to become a triad of law of the Kesdjan Body (illustration 15). At the death of the physical body, the 'individuality' of Kesdjan continues to exist and efforts to complete the Higher Being-body will continue. Implied by *A Symbol* is the *essentiality* of Kesdjan and Higher Being-body in the *completion* of the Lateral Octave.

A certain proportion of three-brained beings must create these two Bodies or the lateral octave will become sterile, relative to its overall purpose to fill the *cosmic* FA–MI interval. Gurdjieff refers (quite obliquely) to the tension that occupies the Higher Bodies in their efforts toward completion.[40]

---

40  Gurdjieff, *Beelzebub's Tales*, p 766.

Another inference from the inner infolding from the triad of a three-brained being to Kesdjan is the relationship to the ultimate genetic origin of a three-brained being. Every man or woman (as a Keschapmartnian being[41]) is a blending of the DNA of a man and a woman. This fact marks each step in the Lateral Octave that a three-brained being passes through. It is a direct reflection of living under 48 orders of law and is demonstrated in his/her second state of consciousness in the yes/no, like/dislike, pleasant/unpleasant nature of the upper notes of the Food Octave.

Kesdjan, however, is a self-creation and does not have the dual nature of the physical body. This is clearly shown by the inward rotation of two triads of a three-brained being to one triad of Kesdjan (illustration 15). In the illustration, two triads (la, three-brained) fold over to blend into one triad at si. Since there are six green triads of three-brained beings (representing the sensory/motor aspect of the three brains in the full enneagram of a three-brained being), the unfoldings point to an emerging simultaneity of law in Kesdjan. The motor aspect of the intellectual being blends with the sensory aspect of the physical being; the motor aspect of the physical being blends with the sensory aspect of the feeling being; the motor aspect of the feeling being blends with the sensory aspect of intellectual being.

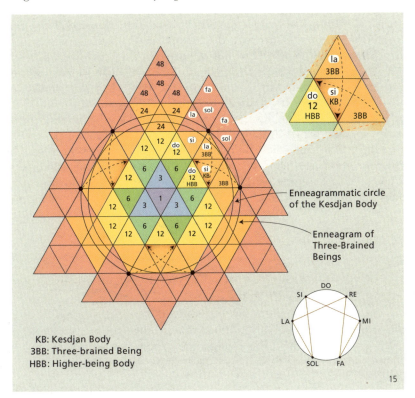

KB: Kesdjan Body
3BB: Three-brained Being
HBB: Higher-being Body

15

41 Gurdjieff, *Beelzebub's Tales*, p 278.

This inward blending – to three simultaneities – is a process totally different and apart from the DNA of the individual. It is a true conscious and intentional blending of aspects of 'oneself', sharing our inner world with 'itself'. It is a *progression to a three,* which lies at the heart of its oneness. A number of the Gurdjieff Inner Exercises and Movements create the conditions for an experience of this type of inner blending.

## The Collapse of the Lateral Octave

Is it possible that the Lateral Octave of this solar system could collapse? It is exactly that possibility that appears to be facing mankind today. The Lateral Octave is a whole; an *organism* of sorts that provides forms and energies that are essential to the Great Ray in the passage through the FA (planetary world) to the MI (Earth). Currently, mankind does not seem to truly understand the consequences of the extermination of species, the degradation of the land and of plant life, the experimenting with one-celled life — and the "naïvely egoistic" misuses of *electricity* (BT, P 1159), both in the outer and inner world of the brain. At least as important is the level of greed, of savagery and narrow convictions that are dominant physical and feeling states in the societies of our world today.

At the same time, it is essential to emphasize the continuing Work that is in manifestation today. It is important to contrast the size of the early Gurdjieff circle of students with the circumstance obtaining in the world today. There are presently thousands of people in many hundreds of groups throughout Europe, both North and South America, Australia and with scattered groups in Russia, Africa and Southeast Asia. There are similar outgrowths from the efforts of Buddhist, Hindu, Christian, Muslim and Sufi leaders and teachers throughout the world. It is obvious that more and more clearly the 'little planet' Anulios is being seen and incorporated in modern fairy tales and in daily life. The primordially important question is whether all of these efforts can alter the course of our present civilization and produce an 'opening' to the inner world of man of sufficient depth and strength to change the present slide toward the dismemberment of the Lateral Octave.

## The Inner-Outer (psycho-physical) Nature of the Laws of World-creation

In science and philosophy, a law is defined as "a formal statement of the manner or order in which a set of natural phenomena occur under certain conditions."[42] Throughout this exploration, we use this definition, qualified by the conditions described by Gurdjieff in his elaboration of the Ray of Creation.[43]

---

42  Webster's Collegiate Dictionary
43  *In Search* chapter 4 and on, and Gurdjieff, *Beelzebub's Tales,* "Purgatory," PP 744-810.

## Pre-Creation — the Principles of Three and Seven

In Gurdjieff's myth of the pre-Creation circumstance, he has HIS ENDLESSNESS concluding, because of the gradual diminishment of HIS Abode (Holy Sun Absolute) caused by the Merciless Heropass, that HE must change the fundamental 'Laws' (Principles) that govern Holy Sun Absolute. The changes in these Principles reflect the Divine Reason of HIS ENDLESSNESS and they will guide the unfolding of the Creation. The Creation Itself is required for the maintenance of Holy Sun Absolute. There must be set in motion a mechanism that will maintain HIS Abode by feeding back energies (forces) that will 'replace' those forces expended from within Holy Sun Absolute in the creation of the Universe. It is also required that Divine-Love and Divine Reason be 'reflected' or 'radiated' *back* to Holy Sun Absolute from created entities — to balance the outflow of these aspects of the Triune Will from within Holy Sun Absolute. The resulting balance (outward from Holy Sun Absolute and inward from the Universe) would maintain HIS Abode without diminishment. The Principles of Three and Seven are the most fundamental of all Laws in that they spell out, at each level of the unfolding Universe, the conditions or circumstances under which secondary laws will operate. In an elemental way, they express Being (the Law of Three) and Becoming (the Law of Seven).

## Heropass

It is our understanding that Heropass is the *infinite potency for all possible motions*. It, therefore, defines all times in the Universe, as Gurdjieff states:

> "... OUR ALL-COMMON MASTER THE MERCILESS HEROPASS ..."[44]
>
> *and* ...
>
> "But as in general, my boy, you do not yet know of the exceptional peculiarity of this cosmic phenomenon Time, you must first be told that genuine Objective Science formulates this cosmic phenomenon thus:
>
> "Time in itself does not exist; there is only the totality of the results ensuing from all the cosmic phenomena present in a given place.
>
> "Time itself, no being can either understand by reason or sense by any outer or inner being-function. It cannot even be sensed by any gradation of instinct which arises and is present in every more or less independent cosmic concentration.
>
> "It is possible to judge Time only if one compares real cosmic phenomena which proceed in the same place and under the same conditions, where Time is being constated and considered.
>
> "It is necessary to notice that in the Great Universe all phenomena in general without exception wherever they arise and manifest,

---

44 Gurdjieff, *Beelzebub's Tales*, p 35, and Buzzell, the chapter "In the beginning, when nothing yet existed," in *Explorations in Active Mentation*, pp 157-63.

are simply successively law-conformable 'Fractions' of some whole phenomenon which has its prime arising on the 'Most Holy Sun Absolute.'[45]

There is, clearly, an infinity of possible motions in our Universe. The possible motions that are 'lawful' in theoretical considerations of the early seconds of our Universe occur as a result of "cosmic phenomena" that involve forces (energies) and speeds that are incomparable to 'motions' that occur in the world of a sun or on a planet like Earth. Each level of the Ray of Creation has its arena of *cosmic phenomena* that define the times of that world. In *Beelzebub's Tales,* Gurdjieff is very careful in to point out the essentials of the vast differences between *cosmic phenomena* (and, therefore, times) that occur in the life of our planet, in the daily life of a man and in the 'daily life' of a bacterium, (*BT,* pp 123-29). He clearly identifies Time as the "'Ideally-Unique-Subjective-Phenomenon',"  (*BT,* p 124). All of these 'Times' and motions must be integrated and harmonized. Gurdjieff refers to this universal process in this way:

> "Well then, these same many hundreds of definite active elements belonging to seven different 'Okhtapanatsakhnian-classes' and having seven different subjective properties – among which the properties of 'vivifyingness' and 'decomposition' have supreme significance – compose in their totality the fundamental common-cosmic Ansanbaluiazar, by which the Most Great cosmic Trogoautoegocrat is actualized – the true Savior from the law-conformable action of the merciless Heropass.[46]      and ...
>
> "And all the results issuing from all the cosmic sources, great and small, taken together, were also then named by them the 'common-cosmic Ansanbaluiazar.'
>
> "It is interesting to remark that concerning this 'common-cosmic Ansanbaluiazar,' present-day objective science has also the formula: 'Everything issuing from everything and again entering into everything.'[47]

This interrelationship within 'All and Everything' makes possible the patterns of involution/evolution that not only relates all levels of the Universe but, at its highest evolutional motion, enters Holy Sun Absolute as a sustaining influence. This entry is the final step in the reconciliation of the Heropass.

The potency for all possible motions (the Heropass) is clearly an expression of the Will Power of HIS ENDLESSNESS[48] and this equivalence raises a question of the relationship between the Divine Will Power and the other

---

45  Gurdjieff, *Beelzebub's Tales,* p 123.
46  Ibid., p 785.
47  Ibid., p 761.
48  Ibid., p 756.

aspects of the Triune Will of HIS ENDLESSNESS, namely Divine-Love and Divine Reason. At the level of World One, these are blended such as to be inseparable. In World Three, we can understand that each Divine Impulse can be considered as distinct.

The Divine Will Power, as Gurdjieff discusses it, is that power (which we consider *is* the Merciless Heropass) that is sent out from within Holy Sun Absolute as the *Emanation*. 'Outside' of Holy Sun Absolute, this Will Power (now manifested as "Okidanokh") is *constrained* (by the two Primordial Principles of Three and Seven) such that even HIS ENDLESSNESS *cannot* alter, by fiat, the processes inherent in Okidanokh.[49] The material Universe will unfold in accordance with successive levels of law which describe and limit what can take place. These 'lawfulnesses' are given form (largely as mathematical formulae) by the varied investigation/experiments of modern science. Statistical probabilities are an important and intrinsic aspect of this 'working out' of the laws – a reflection of the hazards implicit in the Law (Principle) of Seven.

Also to be remembered are the successive levels of 'lawful inexactitudes' which lie beneath the hazards that are manifested in processes now described in Chaos and Complexity theories.

## Symmetry and Creation

> In fact, we will see that the history of the universe is, to a large extent, a history of symmetry. The most pivotal moments in the evolution of the universe are those in which balance and order suddenly change, yielding cosmic arenas qualitatively different from those of preceding eras. Current theory holds that the universe went through a number of these transitions during its earliest moment and that everything we've ever encountered is a tangible remnant of an earlier, more symmetric cosmic epoch. But there is an even grander sense, a metasense, in which symmetry lies at the core of an evolving cosmos. Time itself is intimately entwined with symmetry. As will become clear, the practical connotation of time as a measure of change, as well as the very existence of a kind of cosmic time that allows us to speak sensibly of things like "the age and evolution of the universe as a whole," rely sensitively on aspects of symmetry. And as scientists have examined that evolution, looking back toward the beginning in search of the true nature of space and time, symmetry has established itself as the most sure-footed of guides, providing insights and answers that would otherwise have been completely out of reach.[50]

From Gurdjieff's description of the circumstances obtaining at the level of Worlds One, Three and Six, we can infer that the absolute symmetry of

---

49  Buzzell, *Gurdjieff's Whim*, (Fifth Press: Salt Lake City, 2012), pp 102-42.
50  Greene, Brian, *The Fabric of the Cosmos*, (New York: Vintage Books, 2004), pp 220-21.

World One (where the Divine attributes of Will Power, Love and Reason are perfectly balanced and united as One) has to be 'opened' to the level of World Three in order that Being (the Divine Attributes) be present as a triad of powers. However:

△ Divine-Love, in its nature, requires a 'Beloved', else it is unrequited.
△ Divine Reason must be *expressed*, as, unexpressed, it is infertile; it has no 'field' in which to operate.
△ Divine Will Power is useless (impotent) unless Its power is manifested.

Each of the Divine Attributes has an infinite potency, (potency, in the sense we are using here, is prior even to potential.)

If the Divine Attributes are not expressed but remain in a state of potency only (remaining in a state of perfect symmetry), this would lead, in Gurdjieff's terms, to a diminishment of Holy Sun Absolute. In his myth, this leads to HIS ENDLESSNESS applying HIS Reason and discovering that in the Heropass (HIS own Will Power or potency for all possible motions) is the possible solution. For HIS Will Power to be expressed in its fullness, HE must create a Universe and, for this to be possible, HE must first change the two Principles (Laws of Three and Seven) that maintain HIS Being in a state of perfect symmetry. This act, prior to the Emanation (or onset of the Creation of the Universe), is the introduction of lawful asymmetry. These asymmetries undergo successive levels of manifestation and are responsible for our present understanding and perception of times (moving only 'forward' and not backward), of space (as a three-dimensional reality), of mass and non-mass in all of its intricacies, of the scale of energies, from high gamma waves to ELF waves of the brain. In each instance, as the quote from Brian Greene points out, it is the breaking or opening of a symmetry that results in the contextual nature at multiple levels of our Universe. It is the Principles of Seven and Three, supplemented by the 'secondary' laws which appear at successive levels of the Ray of Creation that describe (in mathematical terms) the results of the breaking of symmetries of law. The Law (Principle) of Seven is the primary 'agent' of this breaking of symmetries, introducing hazard and indeterminacy at every level of existence.

The presence of hazard and indeterminacy, as lawful expressions, force a reassessment of the historical (Biblical) assumptions of *both* omniscience and omnipotence on the part of the Creator. In Gurdjieff's terms, HIS ENDLESSNESS cannot, by HIS own decision, re-enter the Creation with the Will Power. Further, the question asked by Hassein, at the end of *Beelzebub's Tales* (presumptively a question asked by HIS ENDLESSNESS), indicates that there are circumstances in the unfolding of Creation that even HIS ENDLESSNESS cannot anticipate and 'know'. This inference echoes the ancient creation myth wherein the Creator states, as the Universe comes into existence, "let's hope it works!"

The resonance between Gurdjieff's myth (as we understand it) and the findings and theoretical understandings of modern science is quite striking. We consider Gurdjieff's treatment of Time as the most realistic, subtle and comprehensive approach which has been given a form. Rather than a linear, incremental and measured progression that knows no limit, he has removed Time's existence as a single extension (from the past to the future) and given its conception significance in terms of 'cosmic phenomena' at each level of the Universe—quite compatible with the concept of symmetry breaking that marks the progression of law from pre-atomic through atomic, molecular and all aspects of electromagnetic phenomena. Being (the Principle of Three) and Becoming (the Principle of Seven) emerge, in Gurdjieff's conception, as distinct markers of levels of reality in our Universe, introducing a conception that finds remarkable resonances with the concepts of quantum mechanics.[51] Profound reconciliation of West and East is implicit in his presentation in the chapter "Purgatory" of *Beelzebub's Tales*.

## Laws of World 48

The following material has been discussed earlier in this volume. We take it up here for purposes of recapitulation and further development.

The world most familiar to us is the world of bodies and their motions. Your body–my body–the house, chair, car, mountain, river, trees, dogs and squirrels–this is my day-to-day real world. What holds this world together? What Laws determine the 'reality' of the varied bodies?

Gravity stands out as an obvious *rule* or law in our daily life. If we knock a glass off the table, it falls down to the floor, not up. If we lose our balance, we do not fall up. There are, now, formulae (thanks primarily to Newton) that describe the results of this relationship between solid objects. However, if I fall and cut my leg, gravity does not explain the disruption of my bodily surface. What is it that holds 'me' together? For many years, this was a very controversial subject and even now many find the explanation very difficult to grasp. Modern science tells us that it is the electromagnetic bonds between molecules that are disrupted by the impact between the floor and my tissues that causes the cut on my leg. But I cannot *see* the molecule or the 'bonds' that link them. Neither can I *see* the force which causes the glass to fall to the floor. The laws describing these events are quite precise and have been found to be extremely useful in a multitude of circumstances, from building buildings, flying jet planes, to sending rockets to the moon. Unfortunately, we automatically 'forget' that we see neither gravity or electromagnetic forces or molecules!

We set down these two simple examples to highlight the difficulties inherent in trying to discuss the laws of a given world, in this case, the laws of Earth (World 48). This issue becomes even more difficult when we take up the 'laws' that obtain during the digestive octave of the three foods (Food, Air and Impressions, illustration 4, p 27).

---

51 Buzzell, chapter 14, "Gurdjieff and the Quantum World" in *Gurdjieff's Whim*, pp 236-51.

## Food

All of our foods are made up of macromolecular bodies—meaning that they are held together by a complex series of electromagnetic bonds. All of these macromolecules have to be 'taken apart' and this is accomplished by a series of enzymes (and an appropriate level of hydrogen ions, namely, in acidity and alkalinity). Breaking these bonds results in smaller molecules—and heat (as electromagnetic waves). The smaller molecules have greater potential (can enter into many more possible combinations). The end result of this 'taking apart' process (in the stomach and small intestine) is the production of the 'elementals' of simple amino acids, sugars and fats (at MI$_{192}$). The *rules* (or laws) which describe these complex processes are now well known. They are quite precise and, although they have a statistical probability to them (a reflection of the Law of Seven), the end results are predictable within small limits. It never goes in the reverse order—namely, larger, more complex macromolecules are not created by this process.

After the elementals are absorbed across the membrane of the small intestine, this unbonding process is reversed. At FA$_{96}$, the elementals serve as basic building blocks in the creation of the complex proteins, carbohydrates and fats that are unique (because of the unique DNA of the unique body). There are many laws involved in these processes. They are *biochemical* laws that comprise a number of the laws of World 48. Very specific conditions (e.g., temperature, acidity or alkalinity, presence of specific binding enzymes, mixtures of particular building blocks) are required and all of these 'ingredients' must be brought together within the cells of the body where they are acted upon by manifestations of the DNA and the energy systems (ATP) of those cells.

All of these aspects of bodily process, broadly referred to as "biochemistry," are expressions of World 48 laws, although some are directly related to bodily *structures* and some are related to *actions* and are more specifically dependent on ionic-atomic activation. On the World 48 form of *A Symbol* (illustration 9, p 51), the *structures* are aligned to World 48 triads, and the *actions* are aligned to World 24 triads. Both are triads of World 48.

Gravity, as noted earlier, plays a dominant role in World 48 but demonstrates its power more directly as the mass of bodies increases. At the level of atomic-molecular interactions, the gravitational force is extremely weak, having little if any influence on individual, biochemical events. Because gravity has increased expression, as evident law in higher mass-based bodies, it is a major force in the world of Suns (World 12) and galaxies (World Six). It is one of the ultimate unifying forces of our Universe.

*A Symbol* gives visual expression to the progressive increase in the manifestations of law in successive steps in the Ray of Creation as well as showing the integration/appearance of the Laws of Higher Worlds in the lawfulnesses of lower worlds. An example of this integration will help make this point clear. Every atom in every molecule of every 'body' in World 48 (Earth) contains protons and neutrons in each nucleus. Each proton and neutron is 'made' from the confinement of the energy intrinsic to the 3 quarks and 3 gluons that compose these elemental particles. This confinement of energy took place in the first few seconds of the unfolding Creation. As we know from hydrogen bomb explosions, there is extraordinary energy released from the 'unconfinement' of this quark-gluon complex. That energy is still present, in potency, in every proton and neutron in the Universe. The laws of World Six are truly *present* (however, unmanifested) within the laws of World 48!

Establishing gravity and biochemistry as basic laws of World 48 having primarily to do with bodies and structures (organs) and motions, we will now consider the laws that concern the non-mass processes that also take place in World 48. These processes include ionic waves, electromagnetic fields, photons and the Will.

## Brained Beings

The first brain integrates data from the structures of the physical body and from the external senses which report on the structures of the external world as their forms and energies impact the surface of that body. The images produced in the electromagnetic fields of the brain which intimately involve the automatic photonic powers of focus, discrimination and forming patterns–or 8 to 5 on the inner circulation of the physical food enneagram (illustration 7 on P 37)–are reports on the present states of those structures. Data from the internal structures of the body report on the processes taking place–e.g., the need for food of certain types, the presence of inflammation, the state of satiety, vitality and fatigue, the position and motions of bodily parts, the presence or absence of sexual attraction/urges. The external senses result in images of the world at and beyond the body surface–reflecting the macro-molecular and molecular/atomic nature of forms and energies 'out there'.

The first brain gives meaning to these images in terms of:
~ immediate threat to the body–a predator or other physical threat, as in hurricanes or volcanoes;
~ a source of food–a prey or edible plant, berry, etc.;
~ a possible mate–a cyclic expression of reproductive need.

What we call "feeling" is, in the first brain, very close to sensation, e.g., rage, fear, apprehension, satisfaction, hunger and satiety. There are no feeling states that reflect relationship values for *other* in the first brain. It is all centered around survival of the physical body. 'Thinking' functions of the first brain serve the same survival priority. Planning an escape or search involves memory patterns and 'thinking' which can be very clever and resourceful, but these activities have no relation to abstract thought or concept formation about the outside or inside world. By World 48 laws, they cannot create images of relationship with *other*, of value for the 'outside' world other than what serves its survival. The neural systems of the first brain simply do not, cannot, create images other than of survival priorities. We expend a great deal of useless energy 'feeling' guilty or being self-critical when these first-brain priorities are manifested. Better, for a long time, to *see* this manifestation impartially and, as a result, learn how this manifestation is 'put together' or, in other words, to *see* this first-brain law, as it unfolds its triadic nature.

## The Non-Mass Energies

Neural impulses (ionic waves), electromagnetic fields, photonic actions and the Will comprise, from our perspective, the categories Gurdjieff named as 'hydrogens' 48, 24, 12 and 6. These energies (or expressions of Okidanokh) are active in World 48 of the Ray of Creation (Earth) but derive from higher worlds. In Gurdjieff's terms, they are carriers of the laws of higher worlds present within lower worlds (as noted before, of the 48 laws of World 48, 24 laws derive from World 24, 12 from World 12, six from World Six and three from World Three).

Ionic waves 'bond' or join together the world of mass-based particles and the world of electromagnetic fields. In a brain, they are sources of information (data) that flow from one cell to another that are collected together to contribute to the formation of images. The bonding energy derives from the movement of charged particles at right angles to the wave flow itself. Thus, it maintains its energy level throughout its transit. Neural impulses are of great variety and travel at variable speeds, serving direct transmission of sensory data, motor activation to muscles and glands and communication between nerve cells themselves. The many millions of nerve fibers form a dense network, touching nearly every cell in the body. No brained creature is aware of the constant 'motions' taking place in its nervous system. We are aware, to varying degrees, of the results of this immense sharing of impulses.

## Fields and Photons

With the electromagnetic fields of the brain and the role of photons, we enter a highly conjectural area. Scientific investigative techniques have established that there are many, and diffuse, electromagnetic fields within the brain. Their participation in seizure disorders, trauma, tumors, strokes and sleep has been studied for many years. Beyond that, there remain a multitude of unanswered questions. What is the nature of consciousness? How does the brain create images? How do multiple areas in the brain synchronize their functional processes? What is the underlying nature of memory (short-term and long-term)? How do sensations, motions, feelings and thoughts blend together in a present moment of that experience? What is attention? Why do there appear to be many qualities of attention? Why is a feeling subjectively different from a thought or a sensation?

At the present time there are theories, conjectures, convictions and a plethora of isolated observations–but no proven, verifiable conclusions. One point is clear–many of the processes taking place in a nervous system have their origin in biochemical processes and move into the non-mass world of electromagnetic phenomena (all under the laws of World 24). Some of these processes may not originate in biochemistry–like $DO_{48}$ of Impressions, and inquiries must begin in electromagnetic phenomena themselves.

"Biophotons"[52] is a relatively new term that refers to the role of photons (light waves) in biological processes. While the field of investigations is quite young, there are a number of studies that verify:
1) the presence of photonic emissions by living cells and
2) that these photons may play essential roles in conception, cell maturation, differentiation and organ function.

To date these investigations have been focused on visible light photons and not on the ELF (extra low frequency) range of phenomena that are present in brain processes. What roles ELF range photons play is quite conjectural at this point in time. In a perspective that we feel is consistent with Gurdjieff's teaching, we assign photons a primary role in all brained processes and this role is the *attentions*. Gurdjieff's 'hydrogen' 12 category of matter is, like all 'hydrogen' categories, very large and serves specific processes in humans (and other brained creatures).[53]

Photons (H12–the wave/particle carriers of the electromagnetic force) travel at the speed of light, and all have the inherent capacity to focus, differentiate and create patterns (or create 1s, 2s and 3s). Their power, as force carriers, ranges from the immensity of high gamma waves, which are formative/creative powers in the early Universe, to the extremely low power of ELF waves. ELF waves characterize brain photons and are the 'enablers' of the attentions. Naming 'hydrogen' 6 as the Will is speculative and inevitably fraught with controversial assumptions. We have tried to be consistent in our presentation but, as any description of the true nature of all of the forces in the Universe is lawfully bound in the end to be metaphorical, we can only point to what we see as consistencies in our argument.

We feel that these consistencies are resonant representations (images), which are spiritually, scientifically and subjectively demonstrable — in the totality of our experiential life.

## Laws of World 24 in World 48
### Second Brain — Air Octave

The continuance of the Air Octave across the $MI_{48}$–$FA_{24}$ interval is dependent upon what takes place at the $DO_{48}$ of Impressions. This fundamental and essential relationship is taken up by Gurdjieff in some detail in *In Search*. We will focus on this relationship first–and then explore the complexities that he discussed in *Beelzebub's Tales* that deal with the Hasnamuss, because this consideration is critical to our understanding of what may happen at $DO_{48}$ of Impressions. This situation is illustrative of the hazard, which is an intrinsic part of the Laws.

---

52  Bischof, Marco, *Biophotons–The Light in Our Cell* (Frankfurt: Zweitausendeins, 1998).
53  Buzzell, *Reflections on Gurdjieff's Whim*, pp 184-92.

We quote again where Gurdjieff addresses the effort to self-remember, to know and feel that one is present at the DO$_{48}$ of Impressions.

> " ... Moreover, it very often happens that the additional sensation connected with self-remembering brings with it an element of emotion, that is, the work of the machine attracts a certain amount of 'carbon' 12 to the place in question. Efforts to remember oneself, observation of oneself at the moment of receiving an impression, observation of one's impressions at the moment of receiving them, registering, so to speak, the reception of impressions and the simultaneous defining of the impressions received, all this taken together doubles the intensity of the impressions and carries do 48 to re 24. At the same time the effort connected with the transition of one note to another and the passage of 48 itself to 24 enables do 48 of the third octave to come into contact with mi 48 of the second octave and to give this note the requisite amount of energy necessary for the transition of mi to fa. In this way the 'shock' given to do 48 extends also to mi 48 and enables the second octave to develop.[54]

Note that Gurdjieff does not say that it *always* happens that "an element of emotion is brought by the additional sensation connected with self-remembering and then this 'work of the machine' attracts a certain amount of 'carbon' 12 to the place in question." It happens *often*—but not always.

The attraction of 'carbon' 12 (what we understand as *attention*) to the MI$_{48}$–FA$_{24}$ interval "with an element of emotion" is critical to the continuance of the Air Octave. It creates a resonance, a force with an emotional (feeling) quality, between DO$_{48}$ and the MI$_{48}$–FA$_{24}$ interval. A subjective example might be helpful to clarify this 'resonance'.

When I make the effort to remember myself, I may come to the sudden realization that there is a *presence* within that is clearly 'aware of being aware'. At exactly that same moment, I realize that others also can experience this state—that it is a *shared* possibility, in other words, it is not strictly *my own* (in the same way that my bodily sensations are exclusively *mine*). This realization is a powerful feeling (an emotion) that resonates into the MI$_{48}$–FA$_{24}$ interval within me. My attention ('carbon' 12) has been focused on my feeling world (the line from 8 to 5 on the inner circulation) producing a strong sense of *value-for* and *relationship-to others*. When this happens, the MI$_{48}$–FA$_{24}$ interval has been bridged and the Air Octave can continue.

A 'normal' three-brained being can live under 24 orders of laws. All other forms of life (two-brained, one-brained, Tetartocosmos or multi-celled life and microcosmos or one-celled life) live under 48 orders of law. Unfortunately, three-brained beings most often live as two-brained or one-brained beings, totally under the restrictive laws of automaticity (illustration 18a). Once again we give pictorial representation to this circumstance.

---

54 Ouspensky, *In Search*, P 188.

Note that:

1) The Lateral Octave includes all triads enclosed by the orange outlined "Laws of all Life." Each orange form includes two of the six laws which form the octavic steps for each life-form, as illustrated below.

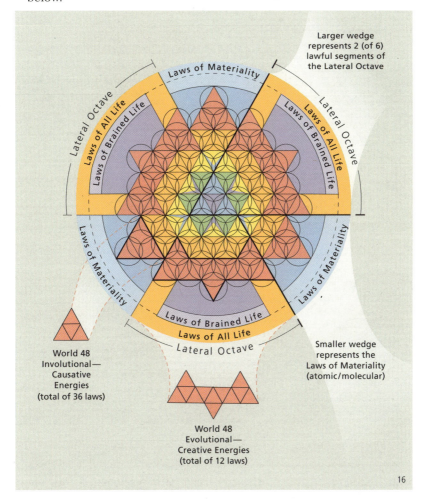

2) Twelve triads of law (red) are in each third of the illustration (one detailed). This makes for a total of 36 triads in the totality of the Lateral Octave. This 36, plus the 12 triads noted in 3) below, make a total of 48 triads of law in World 48.

3) The twelve red triads at the apices of the symbol form, identified under the blue "Laws of Materiality" (one detail shown of the four triads) are those triads of World 48 (red) that derive from triads of law that are determinant (causative/involutional) of the materialities (atomic and molecular) of World 48 (the Earth).

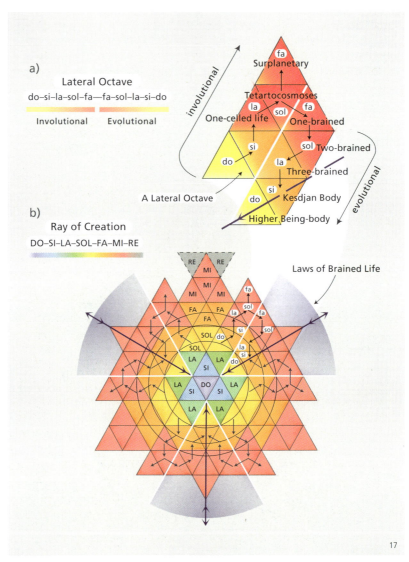

4) Illustration 17a identifies the triads of law associated with one-celled life, Tetartocosmos, plant life, one-brained, two-brained, three-brained, Kesdjan Body and Higher Being-body. Each triad is one of six steps in the enneagrammatic octave of that particular life-form.

5) Within each Lateral Octave (illustration 17b) there are six triads of law of three-brained beings and three triads of law of Kesdjan and Higher Being-body (see illustration 15 on p 65).

6) Illustration 18, includes references to the various photonic energies that play various creative roles. Gamma, X-ray, and high ultraviolet photons lie outside (above in frequency) the triads of life.

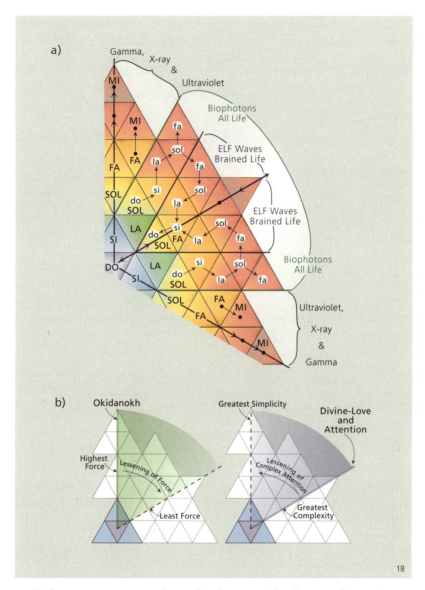

7) There is an inverse relationship between the force and complexity of photonic energies (18 b). The simplest are, simultaneously, the strongest, whereas the most complex have the least force (or energy).

In his description of the derivation of the laws in the Ray of Creation, Gurdjieff includes a representation of the laws of a higher world within the 'laws' of the respective lower world. In consequence, World 48, as a major step in the Ray of Creation, will include 24 laws from World 24, 12 laws from World 12, six laws from World Six, three laws from World Three and three 'of its own.'

How to understand the laws of a higher world within a lower world? Gurdjieff emphasizes that when we come under the laws of a higher world we become 'free' from some of the laws of the lower world. At the same time, coming under the laws of a higher world brings more responsibility for consciousness/conscience.

### Work in the Moment

On the wall of the Study House at the Prieuré a number of Aphorisms were written in a special script of Gurdjieff's design. The following is a selection of these Aphorisms which exemplify 'coming under World 24 law'.

> The chief means of happiness in this life is the
> ability to consider externally always, internally never.

> Only he can be just who is able to put himself
> in the position of others.

> Only he who can take care of what belongs
> to others may have his own.

> If you have not by nature a critical mind
> your staying here is useless.

> Judge others by yourself and you will rarely be mistaken.

> Remember you come here having already understood
> the necessity of struggling with yourself–only with yourself.
> Therefore thank everyone who gives you the opportunity.

> Respect every religion.

> Like what "it" does not like.

It is the world of relationship with *other* that is a primary feature in all but one of these particular Aphorisms (the exception being the emphasis on the need to have a critical mind).

It is our understanding that the effort to fulfill these admonitions is an effort to come under World 24 law. Each of the aphorisms points to a changed state of our inner world, one in which the 'Self' is placed in a lower status and the 'Other' is given preeminence. When one lives in each of life's events in that inner relationship, it could be said that we are living under the laws of World 24 (see the triad of three-brained beings on illustration 17a of the Lateral Octave). This state should be the natural state of a three-brained being (although he or she still is dependent on a physical body, see the shared physical body apex of all three-brained beings with the triads of one- and two-brained creatures, all Tetartocosmoses and Microcosmoses).

In this natural state, a three-brained being has the possibility of creating a Kesdjan Body (see the triad of Kesdjan in its relationship to the triad of a three-brained being–note that two poles of the two triads are shared. The third pole of a three-brained being [the need for a physical body] has 'folded' over, away from the 'need' of a physical body).

One aphorism (the need for a critical mind) points to a different kind of effort on the part of a true three-brained being. This concerns the need to question everything; to 'hunt' for the lawful significance and possibilities underlying life's events. This effort concerns a triad of law of World 12 (within World 48), which involves the digestive Octave of Impressions. This clearly involves the first conscious shock and the establishment of a separate and impartial 'presence'—a step on the long path in the coating process of the Higher Being-body.

We make use of the aphorisms on the Study House wall to point out the very real accessibility of understanding, and functioning within, the laws of higher worlds. The laws of Worlds 24 and 12 (within World 48 of the Great Ray) should not be held to be abstract and unattainably distant in our struggle to Work in accordance with Gurdjieff's teaching. Seeing them as attainable states in our struggles toward Conscience and Objective Reason is important for us to affirm.

### The Lawful Hazard of the Passage from MI48 to FA24

When $DO_{48}$ of Impressions is sounded and there is *not* an element of emotion, which is brought with the effort to self-remember, what is the result? Gurdjieff says little specifically about this circumstance in *In Search* but he takes it up in considerable detail in *The Tales*. In his story that takes up the life of Lentrohamsanin (the chapter, "Destruction of Ashiata Shiemash's Labors," pp 390-410) Gurdjieff discusses in great detail but rather obliquely the possible development of the Impressions Octave when it occurs in the absence of the continuation of the Air Octave. We quote two distinct aspects:

> "The basis for all the further great and small maleficent activities and unconscious maleficent manifestations of the learned beings of that time concerning the destruction of even the last remnants of the results, beneficent for the three-brained beings there, obtained from the very saintly conscious labors of the Essence-loving Ashiata Shiemash, were—as my later detailed researches concerning these further very saintly activities made clear to me—the 'invention' of a learned being, well known there in his time, also belonging to the number of learned beings of new formation and named Lentrohamsanin.

> "As a result of his inner what is called 'double-gravity-centered' existence, the 'highest being-part' of the presence of this terrestrial three-brained being was coated and perfected up to the required gradation of Objective Reason, and later this 'highest being-part' became, as I have once already told you, one of those three hundred and thirteen 'highest being-bodies' who are called 'Eternal-Hasnamuss-individuals' and who have the place of their further existence in the Universe on a small planet existing under the name of 'Eternal-Retribution.' (*BT*, pp 390-91)

"Already by the time this terrestrial what is called 'Papa's-and-Mama's-darling' was approaching the age of a responsible being, he was, as it is said there, very well 'instructed' and 'educated,' that is he had in his presence a great deal of data for all kinds of being 'egoplastikoori,' consisting, as it is usual there according to the abnormally established conditions of their existence, of various fantastic and dubious information; and later, when he became a responsible being he manifested himself automatically through all kinds of corresponding accidental shocks.

"When this later great learned being there reached the age of a responsible being, and although he had indeed a great deal of information or, as it is called there, 'knowledge,' nevertheless, he had absolutely no Being in regard to this information or knowledge which he had acquired.

"Well, when the said Mama's-and-Papa's-darling became a learned being there of new formation, then because on the one hand there was no Being whatsoever in his presence, and on the other hand because there had already by this time been thoroughly crystallized in him those consequences of the properties of the organ Kundabuffer which exist there under the names of 'vanity,' 'self-love,' 'swagger,' and so forth, the ambition arose in him to become a famous learned being not only among the beings of Nievia, but also over the whole of the surface of their planet. (*BT,* pp 394-95)

Note the following:

△ "Double-gravity-center existence" appears to relate to the fact that Lentrohamsanin was focused on the mind (third brain) and the body (first brain) but had no center-of-gravity in his feeling (emotional) brain.

△ His "'highest being-part'" was "coated and perfected up to the that the Impressions Octave can develop—to the required gradation of Objective Reason. How far is that? We feel that there is evidence that he penetrated, in some degree, to $MI_{12}$. Creation of the Kashireitleer is evidence of that. (*BT,* pp 391-402)

△ After being "'instructed' and 'educated'" with data dealing with "fantastic and dubious information" he then, as an adult, manifested himself automatically via all kinds of corresponding accidental shocks. Lentrohamsanin has no consciousness of himself, but reacts to outside stimuli, utilizing only his first and third brains.

△ He has no Being! No progression across the $MI_{48}$–$FA_{24}$ of the Air Octave. He has no Conscience, no feeling for responsible relationships with and to *other*. As a result, he has crystallized within himself those properties of Kundabuffer detailed in the quote.

While Gurdjieff focuses a good deal of attention on Lentrohamsanin as a singular figure, he does so in order to teach us about our own inner world. The passage from $MI_{48}$–$FA_{24}$ of the Air Octave is critical to the development of a balanced three-brained being. Without the emotional (feeling) resonance that can come with efforts to self-remember, the Air Octave cannot pass its MI–FA interval. This circumstance points to the importance of the Itoklanoz (*BT*, PP 438-39) of three-brained beings. Gurdjieff repeatedly emphasized the importance of "good customs and traditions" and this emphasis plays an important role in setting the stage for the resonance between $DO_{48}$ and $MI_{48}$ of Air. An early educational training, which emphasizes *value-for* and *manifestation-of* right relationship with *other*, prepares the soil for the "element of emotion" which attracts the attention of $DO_{48}$ and $MI_{48}$. The bridging of the $MI_{48}$–$FA_{24}$ is far more likely to take place under these normal circumstances.

Gurdjieff placed particular emphasis in *The Tales* (THE ADDITION, PP 1219-1238) on the role of 'accidental' circumstances on the possibility of individual transformation.

We offer a brief quote from these final pages:[55]

> To cross into the other stream is not so easy–merely to wish and you cross. For this, it is first of all necessary consciously to crystallize in yourselves data for engendering in your common presences a constant unquenchable impulse of desire for such a crossing, and then, afterwards, a long corresponding preparation.

△   △   △

## WORLDS 12 AND 24 LAWS IN WORLD 48

We consider the $DO_{48}$–$RE_{24}$–$MI_{12}$ of Impressions to be manifestations of the laws of World 12 operating in World 48. These laws guide the abstracting capacities of the third brain which makes possible the understanding of the laws of the material world of bodies and their motions and the laws of life's purposes and possibilities. This is the underpinning capacity that energizes in particular the various scientific enterprises of the past 400 years. The knowledge, gained through these enterprises, is real but its major weakness is that this knowledge is gained without the participation of the upper notes ($FA_{24}$–$SOL_{12}$–$LA_{6}$) of the Air Octave. The result has been considerable knowledge of the physical (external) world but it lacks meaning and significance in terms of right relationship with all *other—no Conscience emerges from these scientific enterprises*! The realization of real Being, in Gurdjieff's terms, does not take place.

---

55 Gurdjieff, *Beelzebub's Tales*, P 1232.

The first-brain (food) octave, with its focus on the survival of the physical body, when blended in function with the third brain's abstracting capacity, produces a 'system of thought' that lies beneath most of the world's governing/administrating systems with its concentration on political power, influence over 'the masses', weapons of mass destruction war and, above all, survival. All systems that have emerged over time have their fatal flaws.

In music, poetry, dance, drama and other artistic endeavors, we see a partial entry into the feeling world of the second brain. For the most part, however, there remains a focus on the individual (first brain) with its inherent egoism. The result, as Gurdjieff points out, is an art which is subjective, not objective (*not* focused on shared values, the inner world of Being, respect for *other* and Conscience-guided personal responsibility).

The Gurdjieff music, Movements and Sacred Dances are exemplary of objective manifestations of art, blending together the higher 'hydrogens' of the three Food Octaves in an expression of a true three-brained existence. His creations are real examples of "active mentation"[56] to its fullest degree. Since Gurdjieff's death, there has appeared, especially from scientific investigations in the biological sciences, a gradual penetration into the feeling world of the Air Octave. The concerns and actions expressed in the environmental and animal preservation movements are clear indicators of entry into the third state of consciousness, sounding the $FA_{24}$–$SOL_{12}$ notes of the Air (Kesdjanian) Octave and opening into the pursuit of Conscience. These efforts are examples of World 24 laws in operation in World 48.

Exploring the laws of World 48 in the foregoing ways makes it possible to *see* the restrictions of World 48 law in very real and practical ways (relative to Work). The world of the body is clearly under more restrictions than the world of feeling. Analogously, the world of abstract thought is free of many of the limitations of the world of feeling because it can 'view' the world of feeling from an impartial, separated perspective. Understanding the consequences of living under different lawfulnesses simultaneously, as we do in our role as three-brained beings on the planet Earth, creates the possibility that, as we more deeply understand the laws, we become gradually more free of many of them. In turn, and lawfully, we place ourselves under Higher Laws, which requires greater consciousness and efforts toward Being.

## Summarizing Comment
On the following two pages, we will briefly and visually summarize certain common features of our view of the laws of Worlds 96–48–24 and 12.

Emphasized are:

1) The *physical* (material/mass based) consequences of the laws and
2) The *psychological* consequences, which are non-mass based in three-brained beings.

---

56 Gurdjieff, *Beelzebub's Tales*, p 1172.

## World 96

*Physically:*

- ~ A world of rigidity and unchangeableness from within itself
- ~ Strong interatomic and intermolecular bonds–a crystalline, metallic state with no intrinsic energies of self-transformation (aside from radioactivity)
- ~ Gravity is a strong force

*Psychologically:*

- ~ A state of rigidity–in thinking, feeling and motions
- ~ Preservation of the present state; identification and negative imagination; negative emotions.
- ~ A constant defense of the physical individuality

## World 48

*Physically:*

- ~ The world of bodies and their motions
- ~ Moderately strong to weak intermolecular/interatomic bonds (electromagnetic)
- ~ Limited flexibility with preservation of form (it requires higher [ionic] energies to transform form)
- ~ Subject to gravity

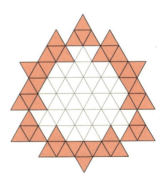

*Psychologically:*

- ~ Uniqueness of the personal body and experience
- ~ No sense of responsibility beyond oneself; all value is in the self
- ~ A world of opposites, with no reconciliation from within itself
- ~ Second state of consciousness (the waking consciousness)

## World 24

*Physically:*
- ~ The atomic and ionic (potential state)
- ~ Remarkable potential within the molecular world–states of tension
- ~ Open to new forms
- ~ Electromagnetic field effects
- ~ Powerful force in atmospheres
- ~ Reconciliation of + (active) and (passive) interactions
- ~ Very little force of gravity

*Psychologically:*
- ~ States of tension between + and –, with real potential for reconciliation
- ~ Inclusion of all *other*
- ~ Struggle 'between two stools' and motion toward Conscience
- ~ Third state of consciousness (consciousness of Being)

## Worlds 12 and Six

*Physically:*
- ~ Creation of atomic elements and powerful ionic states of matter
- ~ Strong gravitational effects–organization of planetary systems
- ~ Creation of simple molecules
- ~ Radiation of life-giving and life-supportive energies
- ~ Initiation and support of all life-forms via the do of the Lateral Octave

*Psychologically:*
- ~ Understanding and enablement of the expression of the laws of Worlds 24–48–96
- ~ Initiation of creative efforts into lower worlds– (e.g., creative imagination, such as the Gurdjieff Movements and music)
- ~ Abstract (objective) images of lawful processes
- ~ Sources of reconciliation of lower worlds with Higher World purposes and possibilities
- ~ Higher Degrees of Reason
- ~ Fourth state of consciousness (objective)

△   △   △

# Hazard

One recurring concept discussed and exemplified by Gurdjieff, in many mythic stories, concerns the lawful presence of hazard (Law of Seven[57]) in life's events. How to be, in the face of the inevitability of hazard, is addressed on two occasions of clear significance. The first occasion takes place shortly after Beelzebub leaves Karatas, accompanied by Hassein, on their long journey to the planet Revozvradendr. Shortly after their departure, the captain informs Beelzebub that, on their present course, they will pass through the solar system 'Vuanik' and that a comet of that system, named the "'Madcap'," will pass through the space of the intended course of the spaceship shortly before they enter this system. The captain says:

> "Your Right Reverence of course knows that this 'Madcap' comet always leaves in its track a great deal of 'Zilnotrago' which on entering the planetary body of a being disorganizes most of its functions until all the 'Zilnotrago' is volatilized out of it.[58]

The hazard obviously lies in the disorganization of most of its (the planetary body's) functions until the Zilnotrago is volatilized out of it. What is this "disorganization?" Confusion and uncoordinated functions and motions would appear to be the consequences of exposure to this hazardous material.

Beelzebub's aim is to get to Revozvradendr and a direct route would expose them to the tail of the comet. The hazard lies in the influence it may have on deflecting their aim. Considering the possible wear and tear on the ship, Beelzebub's decision does not change the direction of their aim, but it does delay them (in time). He elects to wait – and to fill the time of this delay " ... with something useful for us all."[59] As he says:

> " ... when an event is impending which arises from forces immeasurably greater than our own, one must submit.[60]

A most interesting contrast to this episode of potential cometary Zilnotrago is the circumstance faced by Beelzebub when he expresses his desire to the captain to visit the planet Deskaldino and greet the great Saroonoorishan, his first educator. The captain states:

> "Very good, your Reverence, I will think out how it may be possible to carry out your desire. I do not know just what obstacles there were then for the captain of the ship Omnipresent, but in the present case, on the direct route between the holy planet Purgatory

---

57 Bennett, *Hazard*, (Santa Fe: Bennett Books, 1991). We find this book to be particularly useful in understanding the relationship between Hazard and the Law of Seven.
58 Gurdjieff, *Beelzebub's Tales*, p 56.
59 Ibid., p 57.
60 Ibid.

and the planet Deskaldino, there lies the solar system called Salzmanino, in which there are many of those cosmic concentrations which, for purposes of the general cosmic Trogoautoegocratic process, are predetermined for the transformation and radiation of the substances Zilnotrago; and therefore the direct falling of our ship *Karnak*, unhindered, through this system, will scarcely be possible. In any case, I will try in one way or another to satisfy the desire expressed by your Reverence."[61]

The same hazard, of possible exposure to Zilnotrago, is present in this event as was present earlier in their journey. Here, however, Beelzebub decides to take on the risk of disorganization of most of the functions of the planetary body in order to fulfill his proximate aim – and his ultimate aim of returning to Karatas. Why?

Two hazards – one placed close to the beginning of the journey and one placed close to the end. The second is related in the chapter "A Change in the Appointed Course of the Falling of the Transspace Ship *Karnak*," *but* the entirety of the Third Book of *The Tales* still lies ahead. Why place the second engagement with the notion of the 'comet' where he does?

In the second instance the captain notes that " ... the direct falling of our ship *Karnak*, unhindered ... will scarcely be possible."[62] In this instance Beelzebub is prepared to engage in interaction with Zilnotrago. This circumstance presents us with an interesting dilemma relative to our understanding of the inherent hazards of Higher Worlds penetrating into and moving through lower Worlds. We conclude with a quote from Michel Conge:

> As a function of organic life, humanity is linked to the Earth. As an indirect consequence, it will share the Earth's destiny. If the Earth involves, humanity will suffer from it; if the Earth evolves, humanity will experience the repercussions mechanically. But there is nothing to say that these repercussions will necessarily be favourable; organic life may even cease to be necessary. And even if humanity were to benefit, let us not forget that the evolution of the Earth can probably only be assessed in millions, or even billions, of years! This time span, out of all proportion with the duration of an individual human life, ultimately relieves us of any interest in such an uncertain, and moreover problematic, eventuality. What's more, if the chain of consciously evolving men were to be broken, the unguaranteed possibility of an indirect evolution of humanity would come to nothing; if the octave of organic life were interrupted, the higher influences would no longer be able to reach the Earth. As a result, organic life, humanity, the Earth, and the Moon would disappear.[63]

61 Gurdjieff, *Beelzebub's Tales*, p 659.
62 Ibid.
63 Michel Conge, *Inner Octaves*, (Toronto: Dolmen Meadow Editions, 2007) p 22.

## Beelzebub's Aim

We choose to understand the mythic journey of Beelzebub, with the multitude of stories and situations encountered, as Gurdjieff's presentation of his perspective on the entirety of what he terms "Work." In a sense, it can be understood as a journey initiated in the highest world which must penetrate through successive lower worlds, seek out and come to understand the working out of the laws in lower worlds and then provide a means for becoming free of the laws of those lower worlds and ascend (in lawfulness) to the highest of possibilities.

> Growth of understanding becomes hunger for being.[64]

It is a journey that presents hazard at every turn, unexpectednesses during which Beelzebub learns hard lessons about the limitations imposed by the laws of lower worlds. With each descent to Earth, he confronts new difficulties, aspects of laws that place limits on what he can accomplish. In the end, he paints a very multi-colored view of life on Earth, a mix of accomplishments – in Hadji-Asvatz-Troov, Belcultassi and Ashiata Shiemash and a contrasting picture of Lentrohamsanin, war and the misuse of electricity. The hazards of life on Earth are plumbed to the bottom, with a very conditional conclusion reached.

What to make of Salzmanino and the multiple comets lying directly on the path back to Karatas? First, we must see that whatever our individual conclusion may be, we must accept the lawfulness of this hazardous journey. Beelzebub is fully aware that there will be real difficulties, with the disorganization of most of its planetary body functions. Is this a commentary on the inevitable and lawful hazards that Gurdjieff's teaching and methods must go through on the journey toward fulfillment of his aim? However we view this 'event', we must hold to Gurdjieff's final portrayal in "Beelzebub's Opinion of War."[65]

> "But if nothing could be done for the beings of that planet by that Being who now already has the Reason of the sacred 'Podkoolad' and is one of the first assistants of our ENDLESSNESS in the government of the World, namely, the Very Saintly Ashiata Shiemash – if He could do nothing, what then can we expect, we, beings with the Reason of almost ordinary beings?
>
> "You remember the Very Saintly Ashiata Shiemash, then in his deliberations, under the title 'The Terror of the Situation' said:
>
> "'If it is still possible to save the beings of the Earth, then Time alone can do it.'
>
> "We can now only repeat the same in regard to this terrible property of theirs, of which we have just been speaking, namely, their periodic processes of the destruction of each other's existence.

---

64 Jane Heap Aphorism
65 Gurdjieff, *Beelzebub's Tales*, PP 1173-83.

> "We can only say now, that if this property of terrestrial beings is to disappear from that unfortunate planet, then it will be with Time alone, thanks either to the guidance of a certain Being with very high Reason or to certain exceptional cosmic events."
>
> Having said this, Beelzebub again began to look at Hassein with that same strange look.[66]

## Indifference to Cosmic Law

There are three clearly identified chapters in *Beelzebub's Tales* that express *specific opinions* of Beelzebub. These are chapters 43-45.[67] In chapter 47, "The Inevitable Result of Impartial Mentation," Beelzebub is asked and gives his "personal and frank opinion"[68] concerning whether the means are still possible to save the three-brained beings of Earth and "direct them into the becoming path."

These four *opinions* form the capstone of *Beelzebub's Tales* and this requires us to inquire deeply concerning their meaning.

Why should Beelzebub, revealed as a *sacred Podkoolad* manifesting next to the highest degree of Objective Reason possible for a three-brained being, present an opinion?[69] An opinion falls short of an absolute understanding of all laws involved in a given circumstance. If this interpretation is correct, then we are led to the conclusion that all four opinions at the end of *Beelzebub's Tales* demonstrate that even Beelzebub lacked a comprehensive, lawful, understanding of war, justice (good and evil) and the misuse of electricity. We use the expression lawful because, throughout *The Tales*, primary emphasis is placed on Hassein's efforts to comprehend all cosmic laws. In the opening pages of the chapter "Purgatory," Beelzebub put it in these words:

> "...I would answer in such a way, so that I could, apropos, explain to you also what I have already several times promised you to explain.
>
> "That is to say, about the fundamental cosmic laws by which our present World is maintained and on the basis of which it exists; and this moreover should be done, because if both of these questions are taken together, only then will you have all-round material for a complete representation and exhaustive understanding about this holy planet Purgatory, and at the same time learn something more about the three-brained beings who have interested you and who arise on the planet Earth.

---

66 Gurdjieff, *Beelzebub's Tales*, p 1118.
67 "Beelzebub's Survey of the Process of the Periodic Reciprocal Destruction of Men, or Beelzebub's Opinion of War," pp 1055-1118, "In the Opinion of Beelzebub, Man's Understanding of Justice Is for Him in the Objective Sense an Accursed Mirage," pp 1119-1144, "In the Opinion of Beelzebub, Man's Extraction of Electricity from Nature and Its Destruction During Its Use, Is One of the Chief Causes of the Shortening of the Life of Man," pp 1145-1160.
68 Gurdjieff, *Beelzebub's Tales*, p 1182.
69 "a conclusion or judgment held with confidence, but falling short of positive knowledge"

"I wish to give you also now as many clear and detailed explanations as possible concerning this holy planet, as, sooner or later, you will have to know about this, because every responsible three-brained being of our Universe, irrespective of the nature of the causes and place of his arising and also of the form of his exterior coating, will ultimately have to learn about everything concerning this holy planet.

"And he must know all this in order to strive to exist in that direction which corresponds just to the aim and sense of existence, which striving is the objective lot of every three-brained being, in whom, whatever the causes might be, the germ arises for the coating of a 'higher-being-body.'[70]

In the chapter "Form and Sequence," Beelzebub further qualifies his elaboration of cosmic law by restricting the manner of his presentation:

"For this, I have in almost all my tales strictly held to the two following principles:

"The first: not to say anything as if it were my own personal opinion, in order that data necessary for your own convictions should not be crystallized in you in a prepared form according to the opinions of another.[71]

Beelzebub holds to this first principle up to chapter 43, "War." At this point the question "why?" recurs. How is it possible that Beelzebub concluded that it was essential and necessary for Hassein's Oskiano that he, at this approach to the pinnacle point of *The Tales*, give his opinion to his grandson on four of the most elemental issues in the entire *Tales*?

## Outside the Law

We posit that Beelzebub knew that he could not speak from cosmic law in regard to war, good and evil and the misuse of electricity because the ultimate causes of these phenomena lay outside all law. It is *egoism* that lies at the germinal center point of these three pervasive misfortunes to the life of the Earth and it is *egoism* that must be confronted at its root if the underpinning of these three opinions are to be confronted and changed. Beelzebub gives his summarizing opinion directly to HIS ENDLESSNESS at the ending of "The Inevitable Result of Impartial Mentation:"

"THOU ALL and the ALLNESS of my WHOLENESS!

"The sole means now for the saving of the beings of the planet Earth would be to implant again into their presences a new organ, an organ like Kundabuffer, but this time of such properties that every one of these unfortunates during the process of existence

---

70  Gurdjieff, *Beelzebub's Tales*, P 748.
71  Ibid., P 1165.

should constantly sense and be cognizant of the inevitability of his own death as well as of the death of everyone upon whom his eyes or attention rests.

"Only such a sensation and such a cognizance can now destroy the egoism completely crystallized in them that has swallowed up the whole of their Essence and also that tendency to hate others which flows from it—the tendency, namely, which engenders all those mutual relationships existing there, which serve as the chief cause of all their abnormalities unbecoming to three-brained beings and maleficent for them themselves and for the whole of the Universe."[72]

## Egoism and Kundabuffer

Gurdjieff places great emphasis on "the irregular conditions of ordinary being-existence established by them themselves" (*BT*, p 145, and pp 104-05 below):

"Concerning all this it must be said that neither the organ Kundabuffer which their ancestors had is to blame, nor its consequences which, owing to a mistake on the part of certain Sacred Individuals, were crystallized in their ancestors and later began to pass by heredity from generation to generation.

"But they themselves were personally to blame for it, and just on account of the abnormal conditions of external ordinary being-existence which they themselves have gradually established and which have gradually formed in their common presence just what has now become their inner 'Evil-God,' called 'Self-Calming.'

Clearly, Gurdjieff is pointing to an important difference between the crystallized consequences of the organ Kundabuffer and egoism (that which has been established by them themselves). Work, relative to each of these factors, must be very different because the causes lying beneath each one are dramatically different.

## 'Causes' of Kundabuffer

The implantation, by the High Commission, of the organ Kundabuffer was a something ...

" ... caused to grow in the three-brained beings there, in a special way, at the base of their spinal column, at the root of their tail—which they also, at that time, still had ...."

[This, clearly, is a biological process, one ...]

" ... with a property such that, first, they should perceive reality topsy-turvy and, secondly, that every repeated impression from outside should crystallize in them data which would engender factors for evoking in them sensations of 'pleasure' and 'enjoyment.'"[73]

---

72 Gurdjieff, *Beelzebub's Tales*, p 1183.
73 Ibid., pp 88-89.

It also would have taken place after three-brained beings were present on the Earth – a very long time ago. The 'organ' itself was later removed– but we present three-brained beings continue to live under the crystallized consequences of the organ. We repeat the diagram that Gurdjieff presented in *In Search* (P 42), which illustrated 'topsy-turvy' accurately.

| Automaton working by external influences. | Desires produced by automaton. | Thoughts proceeding from desires. | Different and contradictory "wills" created by desires. |
|---|---|---|---|

19

'Reality' becomes defined by the processes originating in the 'automaton working by external influences' (first brain–moving center) and by the 'desires produced by automaton' (mechanical emotions of "pleasure and enjoyment"). The end results are 'thoughts proceeding from desires' and 'different and contradictory "wills" created by desires.' This is a true 'topsy-turvy', with consciousness nowhere to be found and no real choices manifested; it is a totally dependent circumstance. With no consciousness present, one manifestation of automaticity is not aware of (is buffered from) another automatic manifestation. Hence the use of the term "buffer."

### Egoism

A particle of the individual *will* is present from the early appearance of three-brained beings. This is inferred from the following quotation that we have made use of before and is found early in *The Tales*, (P 88).

> "You must know that by the time of this second descent of the Most High Commission, there had already gradually been engendered in them–as is proper to three-brained beings–what is called 'mechanical instinct.'
>
> "The sacred members of this Most High Commission then reasoned that if the said mechanical instinct in these biped three-brained beings of that planet should develop towards the attainment of Objective Reason–as usually occurs everywhere among three-brained beings–then it might quite possibly happen that they would prematurely comprehend the real cause of their arising and existence and make a great deal of trouble; it might happen that having understood the reason for their arising, namely, that by their existence they should maintain the detached fragments of their planet, and being convinced of this their slavery to circumstances utterly foreign to them, they would be unwilling to continue their existence and would on principle destroy themselves.

Clearly, a consciousness ("the attainment of Objective Reason") of their situation is inferred, as, by their being "unwilling to continue their existence," an independent Will is inferred. Here, the other half of the illustration in *In Search* (P 42) is clarifying.

# Third Striving

| Body obeying desires and emotions which are subject to intelligence. | Emotional powers and desires obeying thought and intelligence. | Thinking functions obeying consciousness and will. | I<br>Ego<br>Consciousness<br>Will |
|---|---|---|---|

The 'topsy-turvy' has here been reversed and reality is properly perceived when 'I–Ego–Consciousness–Will' are the true initiators of three-brained functional expression.

It was only the perception, by the High Commission, that three-brained beings would come "too soon" to the realization that their bodily functions served the Moon that could have led to their unwillingness to continue their existence. It is only then that Kundabuffer enters the mythic presentation by Gurdjieff. It was the High Commission's incorrect assumption that led to the implantation that led to the reversal of the initiation of three-brained expression.

## Paradox

Gurdjieff has presented us with a great paradox: the very attribute, which is the most distinguishing and unique 'possession' of every three-brained being *– the core of his individuality and the possible attainment of Objective Reason –* is his *true* Will. At the same time it is, when turned inward in service only to itself, the primary power underlying egoism. Egoism is, in its negative form, the use of 'I–Ego–Consciousness–Will' in service only to itself.

The consequences of the organ Kundabuffer are unconscious and arise from the most mechanical of the functions of the three brains. We *are not* responsible for the presence of the consequences of Kundabuffer in us. We *are* responsible for the *unbecoming behaviors* that flow from egoism.

At the opening to this segment we emphasized that Work, with respect to the consequences of Kundabuffer and to egoism, had to be dramatically different. We hope that the foregoing has made that point clear.

## Work—Kundabuffer

The attainment of real consciousness and the gradual coalescence of the Will are the keys to Work with respect to the consequences of Kundabuffer. The efforts to self-remember and self-observe are essential to the attainment of increasing consciousness and initial utilization of the Will. The inner separation from the manifestations of the automaton are preparatory steps toward true remorse and an increasing understanding of Law (essential steps in the digestive octaves of Air and Impressions).

## Work—Egoism

As Gurdjieff underscores in the ending to "Impartial Mentation," Work with respect to egoism begins with this statement: (*BT*, p 1183)

> "The sole means now for the saving of the beings of the planet Earth would be to implant again into their presences a new organ, an organ like Kundabuffer, but this time of such properties that every one of these unfortunates during the process of existence should constantly sense and be cognizant of the inevitability of his own death as well as of the death of everyone upon whom his eyes or attention rests.

Just as the organ Kundabuffer, its implantation, removal and consequences involved a very long time, it is our understanding that a "new organ" would require a long time to manifest itself completely. The study and verification of our human vulnerabilities and inevitable dissolution are an essential part of that process.

## A Personal Reflection

Because I have to take an aspirin every day, my skin is easily bruised. Several days ago, as I looked at the back of my hand where a large bruise covered much of its surface, I became clearly conscious of the fact that 'I' could do nothing to accelerate the resolution of this bruising. 'I' cannot change the circulation, the movement of cells to clean up the detritus of dead blood cells or the movement of healing hormones and enzymes into and out of the area. I clearly saw that my body is very vulnerable, that it does, automatically via my instinctive center, what it can do—but it will fail at some point and my body will die. My wife was sitting opposite me at that time and I saw, clearly, that she also will die. What, then, of my angers, my judgments, my thinking that I am an important individual? My value for myself, as a singular and important 'self', disappeared—at least for the moment. ... What was left was what could be done to help others. In that moment, nothing else was of any importance.

Is this one way in which we can begin to approach the question of egoism's power?

Approaching the dénouement of *Beelzebub's Tales*, there exists a kind of inverse echo of the circumstance at its very outset.

## The Exile

Gurdjieff's mythic presentation of Beelzebub is a remarkably paradoxical compression of historical perspectives and belief. We quote here the introduction of this remarkable figure in *The Tales*. (BT, P 52)

> Long, long before, while Beelzebub was still existing at home on the planet Karatas, he had been taken, owing to his extraordinarily resourceful intelligence, into service on the "Sun Absolute," where our LORD SOVEREIGN ENDLESSNESS has the fundamental place of HIS Dwelling; and there Beelzebub, among others like himself, had become an attendant upon HIS ENDLESSNESS.
>
> It was just then that, owing to the as yet unformed Reason due to his youth, and owing to his callow and therefore still impetuous

mentation with unequally flowing association—that is, owing to a mentation based, as is natural to beings who have not yet become definitely responsible, on a limited understanding—Beelzebub once saw in the government of the World something which seemed to him "illogical," and having found support among his comrades, beings like himself not yet formed, interfered in what was none of his business.

This portrayal is totally at odds with all prior images of Beelzebub (Ba'al Zabub, Ba'al, Baalzebub or Beelzeboul) in the early Judaic and Christian literature.[74]

These images vary from early Judaic references to the god of Ekron, an ancient Semitic grouping, to a powerful demon, allied with Satan, who possessed great powers of healing. In later Christian literature, Beelzebub has taken on other attributes. The imaginative works of the 16th and 17th century occultists portrayed Beelzebub as, variably, revolting against the Devil, being the chief lieutenant of Lucifer and being among the most prominent fallen angels. John Milton, in Paradise Lost (1667), characterized Beelzebub as the second ranking of the fallen cherubim, and he is mentioned in Bunyan's *Pilgrim's Progress* (1678). It is from these sources that the majority of the population of the Western world have 'inherited' the characterization of Beelzebub as an icon of Evil (in the artificial division of higher powers into Good and Evil).

It is evident that Gurdjieff chose his 'hero' with considerable care and awareness of the paradox he was creating in the mind, feeling and body of the reader of *Beelzebub's Tales*. Most essential, we feel, is his emphasis on the independence of Beelzebub's Will in his manifestations on Holy Sun Absolute. Beelzebub is young, inexperienced, brilliant and very assertive. He is wholly committed to the conclusions his young mind has arrived at and his perception of something illogical in the government of the World leads him to share his conviction with his 'comrades'. His error is the result of inexperience and poor judgment and in no way is the result of an 'evil' will—a will indifferent and opposed to the WILL of HIS ENDLESSNESS. He accepts the decision/judgment of HIS ENDLESSNESS regarding his exile, and we are given no indication that he thought of rebellion or coming into direct conflict with the One Will. This assertion of his Will is an essential characterization of the independent Will—a *particle* of which is given to all three-brained beings.

It is of fundamental importance that we see, clearly, what Gurdjieff is so emphatic about in the story of the Exile. Each of us has a particle of the independent Will and, in seeing this, we can see directly into the core of egoism. If this Will turns against the WILL of HIS ENDLESSNESS, becoming indifferent to cosmic law and wholly absorbed in self-gratification and the

---

74 References: Rudwin, Maximilian, *The Devil in Legend and Literature*, 2nd Edition, NY, 1970. Also Volume 1 of *Anchor Yale Bible Dictionary; Catholic Encyclopedia; Jewish Encyclopedia; New Bible Dictionary* (3rd edition).

pursuit of "'naïvely egoistic' aims,"[75] then we have the circumstance addressed in Beelzebub's "personal and frank opinion" at the end of "The Inevitable Result of Impartial Mentation."

During the second descent to Earth, Beelzebub gives final voice to this issue of the individual, independent Will and the WILL of HIS ENDLESSNESS when he says:

> "After these Sacred Individuals had left the planet Mars, I decided to carry out the said task at all costs, and to be worthy, if only by this explicit aid to our UNIQUE BURDEN BEARING ENDLESSNESS of becoming a particle, though an independent one, of everything existing in the Great Universe.[76]

In this statement is confirmation of Beelzebub's continued dedication to the blending of his Will, to dedicate this singular, independent attribute, to serving the One Will.

## Singular Issue

From one perspective, it is possible to view the entirety of *Beelzebub's Tales* as a study and mythic presentation of Gurdjieff's view on the most primary of issues confronting mankind — that of the inherent paradox of the Will. The three 'opinion' chapters, which encapsule the end of *The Tales*, and the final opinion rendered to HIS ENDLESSNESS ITSELF, confirm this perspective on Gurdjieff's view. It seems incumbent upon each of us to confront this paradox which lies deeply buried within each of us.

## Obyvatel

The discussion of the Obyvatel (*ISM*, PP 362-65) is interesting with respect to an exploration of Law. Earlier (*ISM*, PP 45-50, 91-4) Gurdjieff, in discussing the four ways, places general mankind in a very restrictive category as regards the possibility of individual evolution. It is essentially impossible for a person under the mechanical conditions of everyday life to come, *individually*, to coalesce a higher Body (Kesdjan or Higher Being). The four ways represent the only 'ways' for man to escape the laws of Worlds 24–48. However, in the material on Obyvatel, clear reference is made to the possibility of individual evolution 'outside' the four ways. How to account for this rather significant difference in perspectives?

One way of approaching this difference is to look on them as expressions of laws, but in different *worlds*. The initial discussion is presented quite early on in *In Search*, when the members of the group were quite 'young' in the Work and Gurdjieff presented the ideas of the four ways within the context of the laws of World 48 (and perhaps of World 24). The laws in this world (48)

---

75 Gurdjieff, *Beelzebub's Tales*, P 1159.
76 Ibid., P 183.

have a certain 'arena' of *possibilities*. They are quite constricted with rather sharp divides in the possibilities for man. When one lives in this world, this is all that can be 'seen' or understood.

When one's understanding begins to penetrate into the laws of World 12, a great enlargement in *possibilities* takes place. However rare they may be, the possibilities for certain Obyvatels (the good, essence-strong and practical type) to individually evolve along their own individual path are real.

Speaking in terms of World 48 law, it is correct and true to say, "There are only four possible 'ways' to immortality," as Gurdjieff does early in *In Search*. Later, speaking more in terms of World 12 law, it is correct (and true) to enlarge man's possibilities and include a uniquely *individual* possibility.

If we (*for the moment*) accept the *differences* in possibilities as a feature which differentiates World 48 law from World 12 law, we can ask other interesting questions. For instance, the materialities and energies (atoms, molecules, bonding energies) that operate in World 48 are totally different from the 'materialities and energies' (electromagnetic waves, fields and photons) of World 12. Bennett's approach (*essence* being non-mass, and *existence* being mass-based) places the *form* of the 'lower' laws in World 12 as … O (essence) — O (essence) — X (existence–mass-based). The boundary between the mass-based worlds of atoms/molecules is creatively breached at a solar level, in that the creation of the atomic table of elements is a 'work' of suns. There is an infinity of possibilities in this unfolding of the atomic table – with all the possible combinations appearing which produce unpredictable and utterly new (novel) forms of relationship (think of what water – $H_2O$ [a combination of H and $O_2$]– means in Worlds 24–48!).

The planetary World (24) of our solar system is a vast 'working out' of the world of atoms and molecules and electromagnetic energies. Each planet (Mercury, Venus, Earth, Mars, Saturn, Jupiter, etc.,) is a realization of *possibilities*, balanced by the forces deriving from the Sun. The Earth is unique (truly novel) in that it is a specific state of 'wind, waves and rocks' that created the *possibility* that Life could emerge. This is a colossally significant 'uniqueness', in that it makes possible the filling of the FA–MI interval of the Great Ray. The Lateral Octave emerges as an enormously significant 'exploration of possibilities'–and the role of *man*, in the completion of this octave, is critical to the entirety of the Great Ray. The 'Idea' (the process of Reasoning) behind the Lateral Octave is an exploration of *possibilities*. No guarantee of its success is present. It will take persistent and great Work to bring the Lateral Octave to its possible fulfillment. The 'Idea' has to be seen from the level of the Sun (World 12) and the understanding of the laws of that world must be wholly integrated into the effort.

The digestive process in the Octaves of Air and Impressions is, essentially, an exploration of *possibilities*. The $MI_{48}$–$FA_{24}$ of Air presents possibilities for manifesting 'images' of pure emotions (Gurdjieff's term for emotions resulting from Higher Emotional Center function grounded in Conscience). At the level of $SOL_{12}$, the *creative* potential is explored as the coating process of Kesdjan takes place. Exactly how this 'image' of higher emotion is manifested is a uniquely individual enterprise, as we see in the lives of the 'saints' and other extraordinary individuals. They are each resonant with the lawful possibilities of World 12.

At $MI_{12}$, the 'elementals' of Higher Being-body are produced. This would include an understanding of the 'lawful' construction of 'Is' down to their *elemental* components and the exploration of possible manifestations (via active mentation) that would be most helpful for *other*. A *consistency* (a reflection of Real I—a *unique* individuality at $FA_6$) would be present, in that all manifestation (physical, emotional, intellectual) would have, at its core, a devotion to HIS ENDLESSNESS and to service to 'everything that breathes'. The Higher Being-body thus created would be both unique (an *arising* from below) and cosmic (conjoined with the WILL of HIS ENDLESSNESS in the fulfillment of the Lateral Octave).

The 'elimination/transformation' of negative emotions is a particularly unique exploration in the passage of $MI_{12}$ across the second conscious shock to $FA_6$. The recognition and verification of my 'nothingness' is fundamental to this transformative process. My egoism is, at its core, based on the 'belief' that I am, as I see myself, a 'something' of significance in this Universe. When seen from the level of World 12, my false 'individuality' disappears in the plethora of possibilities that unfold from the level of the sun. The *physical* individuality of 'myself' disappears in the billions upon billions of life-forms that appear in the Lateral Octave. What is left of my mechanical and negative manifestations and perspectives? I see them all as *constructions* (as false 'creations') of the automaton that is 'myself'.

The artificiality of the false 'creation' is obvious when seen from the perspective of World 12 law. The elementals, however, remain as the 'bits and pieces' that are to be recreated into the *Body* of Higher Being. Here, *choices* must be made as to how we are to manifest (physically, emotionally and intellectually). We can *choose*, in this true creative effort, what emotion or feeling state is to be placed in this particular triad of I at $FA_6$. If the choice is infused with the 'service to the One Will' (which comes from the $H_{12}$ 'substance' which enters at this $MI_{12}$–$FA_6$ interval from *outside* [from ENDLESSNESS ITSELF]), then the uniqueness of Real I will appear. I choose to think that it is possible to see, in Gurdjieff's many daily manifestations when he is 'teaching', this near instantaneous *choosing* of how to manifest for the benefit of *other*. (Quoting Gurdjieff at the Prieuré, August 12, 1924)

> If you help others, you will be helped, perhaps tomorrow, perhaps in a 100 years, but you will be helped. Nature must pay off the debt. ... It is a mathematical law and all life is mathematics.

We are each extremely complex organisms; as Gurdjieff says, the passage from $MI_{12}$ to $FA_6$ is a lengthy one, with a nearly infinite array of negative states that are to be transformed. Only the understanding of law from the level of World 12 makes the 'creation' of Higher Being-body possible.

The harmonization of electromagnetic rhythms, which may underlie these changes in the state of consciousness, might make possible an entirely different level of functioning of the nervous system, in which the mechanisms of perception are no longer confined by ordinary neuronal signaling, limited to meters per second, but function in part at the speed of electromagnetic wave propagation, at light speed. The "light of consciousness" may be more than a metaphor.[77]

Everything in the world obeys the Law of Three, everything existing came into being in accordance with this law. Combinations of positive and negative principles can produce new results, different from the first and the second, only if a third force comes in.[78]

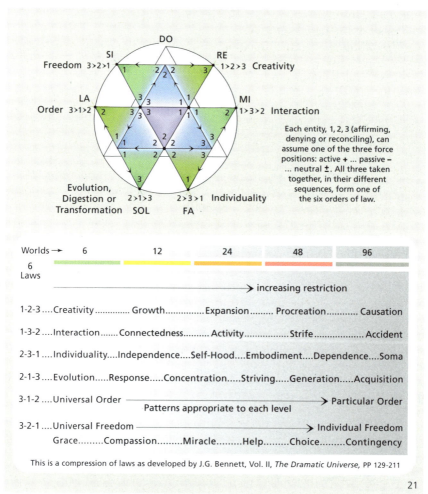

[77] Wertenbaker, *Man in the Cosmos*, p 74.
[78] Gurdjieff, *Views from the Real World*, p 195.

△ △ △

## THE PARADOX OF ATTENTION AND WILL POWER: 'SEEING' AND 'DOING'

In Gurdjieff's myth concerning the creation of the Universe, the Divine Attention is what discovers the gradual diminishment of the Holy Sun Absolute, looks deeply into the laws governing the Holy Sun Absolute, discovers that it is "merely the Heropass" that is responsible for the diminishment and then goes deeply into a study of the laws to find a solution. That solution involves,

△ changing the laws of Triamazikamno and Heptaparaparshinokh and ...
△ directing the Will Power (emanating) "... from within Holy Sun Absolute, out into the 'space' of the Universe ...."(BT, p 756)

In Gurdjieff's elaboration of Creation there is a clear distinction between the Divine Attention (the highest degree of Reason) that makes possible the understanding of the cause and means of resolution on the one hand—and the Will Power to initiate the creative process on the other.

Two attributes of the triune state of World One are referred to here. The third attribute, Divine-Love, is not referred to specifically in the chapter "Purgatory." It is noted, specifically, in two other places in *The Tales* (pp 124, 370). It seems evident that it is the attribute of Divine-Love that reconciles the attributes of Divine Reason (Attention) and Divine Will Power, (illus. 22).

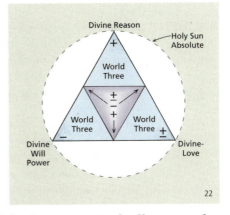

22

At the level of World One, the three Attributes are inseparable, being, simultaneously—all three—in a state that is impossible for us to truly visualize or feel. We can grasp some notion of this simultaneity of attributes when we consider World Three (Holy Sun Absolute). Here, the three attributes are separable and this appears to be how Gurdjieff spoke of them.

When looked upon as separate attributes, it is possible to see a resonance between the triune Attributes of Reason, Will Power and Love and the description Gurdjieff uses in referring to the Law of Three (Triamazikamno). The Holy-Affirming is Reason and is analogous to our third brain; the Holy-Denying is the Will Power and is analogous to our first brain (physical body brain); the Holy-Reconciling is Love and is analogous to our second (emotional) brain.

Man becomes truly an image of the Megalocosmos[79] (HIS ENDLESSNESS) if he evolves to the level of having a Real I (analogous to World One) with a triune 'nature' of Higher Intellect (third brain), Kesdjan, (second brain) and physical body (first brain) in a true, harmonious relationship.

---

79 Gurdjieff, *Beelzebub's Tales*, p 775.

# Third Striving

## The Separation of Divine Attributes in the Unfolding of Creation

One way of giving a visual form to the expression of the Divine Attributes in the creation of the Universe is via a triadic representation, *A Symbol of the Cosmos and its Laws*; it is constructed on the principle of triadic unfolding that successively doubles the triadic expression of laws in each World. Beginning from a single triadic expression of World One, it 'unfolds' to these triads –> World Three, (illustration 23).

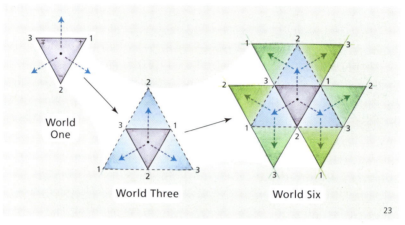

23

With this simple scheme it becomes possible to unfold a symbol form that has had considerable usefulness in our efforts to study the laws of the unfolding Ray of Creation in triadic form.

The requirement that the number of laws *double* with each World led to the form for World Six. Note the following:

1) The unfolding from World One –> Three –> Six proceeds by unfolding over a **side** of the triad.
2) The form of each of the laws follows this triadic sequence:
   ~ First force is that apex which is shared with World One
   ~ Second force is that apex which is shared with outer apex World Three
   ~ Third force is that outer apex which unfolds from the opposite apex of Worlds Three–One, (illustration 23).
3) Carrying out this approach produces 6 mirrored triadic representations:
   1 2 3 <-·-> 3 2 1,   1 3 2 <-·-> 2 3 1,   2 1 3 <-·-> 3 1 2, (illus. 24).
4) The 6 triadic representations have been taken to represent the six laws of World Six discussed by J. G. Bennett.

The World Six form raises interesting considerations.

△ The unfolding, to this point, has been over the **side** of a triad. There is an implication of 'greater surety or stability' in this type of unfolding, compared to an unfolding (as yet not seen) over an **apex** of a triad.

△ If the next unfolding is carried out, moving toward a triadic representation of the laws of World 12, an interesting issue concerning ***apical*** unfolding emerges, illustration 25 b).

# Paradox: Attention–Will Power

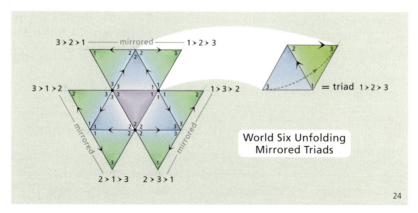

24

The six yellow World 12 triads, 25a), derive from World Six triads and could, thereby, be considered to represent the six laws of World Six *in* World 12. This leaves three triads of law from World Three and three triads of law from World One (the *three of its own*) unaccounted for to this point. And this brings our consideration to the **apical** unfoldings. Visually, an apical unfolding does not appear to be as 'secure' as a side unfolding, introducing the possibility that the lawful expression in that world could have an *indeterminate* or *hazardous* aspect to it. The final *form* of World 12 law is shown on 25b.

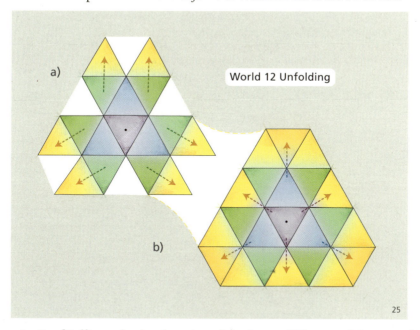

25

In Gurdjieff's myth, the changing of the Laws of Three and Seven took place within Holy Sun Absolute, *prior* to the Emanation of Theomertmalogos. The World 12 triads, then, represent the laws that reflect the *process* of the Creation of the Universe. (*BT*, pp 756-59)

# Third Striving

The *origin* of the laws deriving from World Three and World One are of particular interest. The Emanation (via the Will Power) derives directly from World Three. The *Divine Attention*, however, we assume derives directly from World One. The contrasting origins of two of the infinite potencies of the Triune nature of World One is of great importance.

## Okidanokh and the Ray of Creation

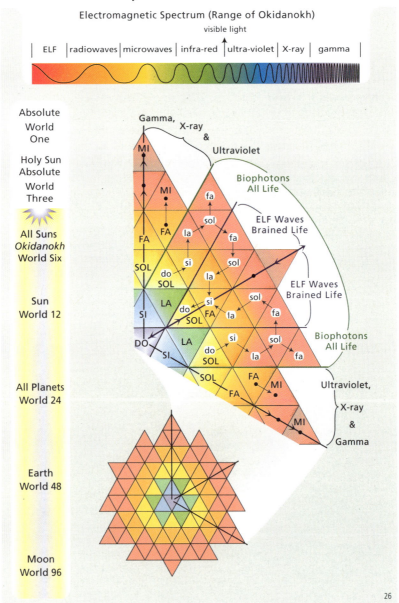

## PARADOX: ATTENTION–WILL POWER

The Will Power (referred to as Okidanokh when it manifests outside of Holy Sun Absolute) undergoes progressive *decrease* in vibration as passage down the Ray of Creation takes place. The highest rate of vibration (Gamma waves) is intimately involved in the creation of the mass-based world of nuclear components (quarks, gluons, protonic nuclei, electrons, etc.,). The energetic wave forms of lower Gamma, X-ray, ultraviolet, visible light, microwave, radio wave and ELF (extremely low frequency) are those energies that determine the successive levels and types of *interaction* that take place at each step of the Ray of Creation.

The *decreasing* rate of vibration is essential to emphasize. By the time the rate of vibration reaches the ELF range, there is very little or no Will Power. The photons in this range still travel at the speed of light, but with crest-to-crest distances in these wave forms that are extraordinarily long (reaching tens of thousands of miles), there is little or no energy-of-action (force or Will Power).

The *Symbol* form illustrates this progressive diminishment in frequency and power to incite change/interaction.

The point we wish to emphasize here is that the Divine Attention (emerging from World One apices) has *very little* or *no* energy-of-action or Will Power to *change* anything. By inference, IT can 'see' and 'understand' every lawful process in the Universe, but IT *cannot change* any of those lawful expressions (see illustration 19b on P 79).

The singular question that arises, then, is "how can real transformation take place?" If the Will Power is unchangeable in its lawfulness, and the Divine Attention is essentially *powerless* in its expression, how then can we understand and resolve the resultant paradox?

### The Role of Divine-Love

The reconciliation of the dilemma, *no* energy-of-action, lies in the Reconciling Force of the Triune nature of World One (HIS ENDLESSNESS).

It is via the Reconciling Force of Divine-Love that the Will Power and Divine Attention can be brought into a *shared* and *resonant* relationship. However, where we three-brained beings exist, very far from the influence of World One, we cannot claim to have direct access to this attribute of the Triune Will. The best we have, according to Gurdjieff, is our *wish* or desire.

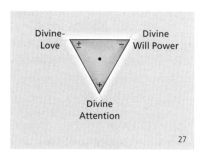

27

... 'Will' is absent in ordinary mechanical man, he has desires only; and a greater or lesser *permanence* of desires and wishes is called a strong or a weak will.[80]

---

80 Ouspensky, *In Search*, P 42.

## Third Striving

We have gathered quotations, from *Views from the Real World* (New York: Dutton, 1973) and the first quote is from Jane Heap (manuscript from her personal papers), which focus on the essentiality of wish.

If you "wish," you "can." Without "wishing," you never "can." Wish is the most powerful thing in the world. Higher than God. With conscious wish everything comes.

To govern oneself is a very difficult thing—it is a problem for the future; it requires much power and demands much work. But this first thing, to separate oneself from oneself, does not require much strength, it only *needs desire, serious desire*, the desire of a *grown-up man*. (*Views*, p 148, [author's italics] and the following):

Before being able, one must wish.
Thus, there are three periods: to wish, to be able, and to be.
The Institute is a means. (p 153)

Working on oneself is not so difficult as wishing to work, taking the decision. (p 222)

Now, when an unpleasant sensation in the body, especially in certain places, has already resulted, I begin to think in my mind: "I wish. I wish very much to be able often to recollect, in order to remember that it is necessary to remember myself. I wish! You—it is me, it is my body." I say to my body: "You. You—me. You are also me. I wish!" (p 233)

This possibility [to pass from one river to another] depends on desire, strong wish of a very special kind, wishing with the essence, not with the personality. (p 247)

You wish to change, but which part of you has this wish? Many parts of you want many things, but only one part is real. ... Sincerity is the key .... (p 248)

[A teacher can only help you] ... when you wish in the right way. ... So, we must have as our aim the capacity to wish, and this can only be attained by a man who realizes his nothingness. (p 249)

One of the best means for arousing the wish to work on yourself is to realize that you may die at any moment. But first you must learn how to keep it in mind. Aphorism #33 (p 283)

### Wish and Love

How can we understand wish as an expression of love in our world–so far removed from the Divine-Love of World One? In its purest, most non-egoistic form, what do I wish for? If I accept my nothingness and I realize that I may die at any moment, what do I wish for? And how to understand that this wish is a form of love?

To wish to have Being, I must *value*, even *treasure*, that state of Being. Intellectually, as Belcultassi did, I *see* that he ...

" ... sensed and cognized that the process of the functioning of the whole of him had until then proceeded not as it should have proceeded according to sane logic."[81]

He reacted to this emotionally—this resulted in the following:

"This unexpected constatation shocked him so profoundly that thereafter he devoted the whole of himself exclusively to be able at any cost to unravel this and understand.

"First of all he decided to attain without delay such a 'potency' as would give him the strength and possibility to be quite sincere with himself, that is to say, to be able to conquer those impulses which had become habitual in the functioning of his common presence from the many heterogeneous associations arising and proceeding in him and which were started in him by all sorts of accidental shocks coming from outside and also engendered within him, namely, the impulses called 'self-love,' 'pride,' 'vanity,' and so on.[82]

What could it infer that "he devoted the whole of himself?" It clearly demonstrates that he greatly *valued* what he "sensed and cognized." He had real *wish* (an *essence wish*) to understand why his inner world was so 'illogical'. This is an example of a simultaneity of intellectual/emotional perception and response to the state of his inner world. We propose that this essence *wish* is an act of love, an expression of that which is cherished and supported. The effort to "... attain without delay such a 'potency' as would give him the strength and possibility to be quite *sincere* with himself ..." (author's italics) is a clear expression of a wish to maintain an inner separation between the I which sees and the multitude of 'Is' that reflect the impulses of self-love, pride and vanity, etc..

The essence, untouched by Kundabuffer or its consequences, is present within the third state of consciousness (its Being). The "shock" spoken of in the quotation is clearly the first conscious shock.

The attainment of the state of Conscience is the primary aim of the Akhaldan society. Its leader, Belcultassi, attains the "... perfecting of his higher being part to the Being of a Saint 'Eternal Individual'." This attainment is, simultaneously, the result of a great and prolonged effort and an act of love, resonant between World One and the essence wish of Belcultassi. It demonstrates the remarkable power of *real wish* which functions as the Reconciling Force between Reason and the Will Power.

This reconciliation—between Divine Reason and Divine Will Power—is clearly expressed in Gurdjieff's "Friendly Advice" at the opening of *Beelzebub's Tales*. On the following page, we quote the last paragraph of his Friendly Advice: (*BT*, front matter)

---

81  Gurdjieff, *Beelzebub's Tales*, p 295.
82  Ibid.

"Read each of my written expositions thrice:
Firstly—at least as you have already become mechanized to read all your contemporary books and newspapers.
Secondly—as if you were reading aloud to another person.
And only thirdly—try and fathom the gist of my writings."
Only then will you be able to count upon forming your own impartial judgment, proper to yourself alone, on my writings. And only then can my hope be actualized that according to your understanding you will obtain the specific benefit for yourself which I anticipate, and which *I wish for you with all my being*. [author's italics]

Gurdjieff's love of humanity, of all life, is explicitly manifested in this 'essence wish.'

## Wish and Choice

Love (or essence wish) reconciles Reason and Will Power by blending the two together via choice. For example, if I, like Belcultassi, have a real wish to be sincere in my evaluation of my inner world, I must *choose*, again and again, not to give into my self-love, vanity, etc., but to remain separated and impartial to what I see. My reason leads me to see that my inner world functions not "according to sane logic." I bring my will into action by *choosing* to make effort toward sincerity. But I must make this effort again and again because,

~ my will is quite weak, and
~ there are many hundreds of inner world happenings, which have to be impartially dealt with.

By repeating the effort, *again and again*, my Will will grow stronger—but only if I hold-to-my-wish-to-be sincere. My reason also increases via this repeated action, as I 'see' over time more deeply into the origins of my self-love, vanity, etc..

## The Ways

In the previous segment, we noted Gurdjieff's emphasis on the *possibility*, within World 12 laws, of real transformation for an individual. This possibility lies 'outside' of the four 'Ways' and *begins* at the level of the 'good' Obyvatel. With real essence wish, a very high possibility opens for an individual at the level of the Obyvatel. The essentiality of the *real wish* is what we emphasize here, because a real wish is not the exclusive possession or 'property' of any one path. It can be expressed by individuals raised in any, or none, of the Great Traditions. It is incumbent on us, of the Fourth Way, to be tolerant and supportive of *all* efforts to move into "the becoming path."

## Consciousness — A Precondition for Love

Gurdjieff specifically categorizes three types of love, (*BT*, p 361):

> Love of consciousness evokes the same in response
> Love of feeling evokes the opposite
> Love of body depends only on type and polarity.

Further qualification can be drawn from these quotations (regarding the Breasts of a virgin of the Akhaldan symbol):

> "… expresses that Love should predominate always and in everything during the inner and the outer functionings evoked by one's consciousness … (*BT*, p 310)   and …

> "… in none of the ordinary beings-men here has there ever been for a long time, any sensation of the sacred being-impulse of genuine Love. (*BT*, p 357)

Consciousness, as Gurdjieff applies the word in the above quotations, is used in reference to the *third* state of consciousness, that is, that state which follows on the first conscious shock (illustrated below).

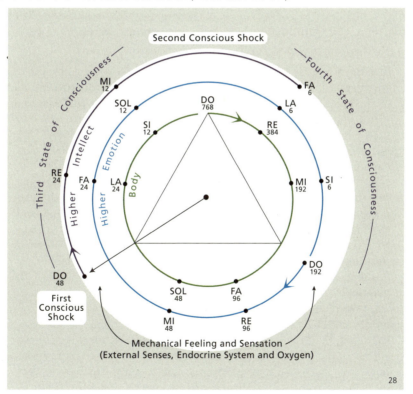

The "sacred being-impulse of genuine Love" enters *potentially* at $DO_{48}$ and $FA_{24}$ with the first conscious shock. This impulse is *expressed* as a real wish.

### A Lifetime of Effort

The effort to initiate the first conscious shock is the *beginning* of a lifetime of struggle, impartial perception, choice and a multitude of failures. The moments of 'presence', of some aspect or degree of self-remembering, are, for a long time, so *brief*, that nothing is transformed in our inner world. Gurdjieff's emphasis on a three-brained being's lack of Will is a *very difficult pill* to swallow; with many misunderstandings of what Gurdjieff was pointing to. A significant aspect of this misunderstanding derives from our failure to understand and accept the biological laws that have their influence well *below* our ordinary level of consciousness. For example, when Gurdjieff speaks of the involution of Exioëhary, we understand that he is referring to the 'descent' (or involution) of the *attentions*, resulting in a focus on the automatic expression of sexuality, survival, self-pleasure, dominance, etc.. The emphasis on involution is important to explore. Exioëhary (Attention) is the highest and most refined energy ('hydrogen') produced by the digestive processes of physical food. It should be utilized in the highest functions of the *body* (reproduction, maintenance of health, learning of skills, complex motor movements and sensing). Unfortunately, this highest of physical energies, when it *involves*, brings a high level of energy into contact with a non-conscious aspect of the automaton. Gurdjieff discussed this with great clarity. (*In Search*, P 258)

> "This is the 'abuse of sex.' It is necessary, further, to remember that the sex center works with 'hydrogen' 12. This means that it is stronger and quicker than all other centers. Sex, in fact, governs all other centers. The only thing in ordinary circumstances, that is, when man has neither consciousness nor will, that holds the sex center in submission is 'buffers.' 'Buffers' can entirely bring it to nought, that is, they can stop its normal manifestation. But they cannot destroy its energy. The energy remains and passes over to other centers, finding expression for itself through them; in other words, the other centers rob the sex center of the energy which it does not use itself. The energy of the sex center in the work of the thinking, emotional, and moving centers can be recognized by a particular 'taste,' by a particular fervor, by a vehemence which the nature of the affair concerned does not call for. The thinking center writes books, but in making use of the energy of the sex center it does not simply occupy itself with philosophy, science, or politics–it is always fighting something, disputing, criticizing, creating new subjective theories. The emotional center preaches Christianity, abstinence, asceticism, or the fear and horror of sin, hell, the torment of sinners, eternal fire, all this with the energy of the sex center. ... Or on the other hand it works up revolutions, robs, burns, kills, again with the same energy. The moving center occupies itself with sport, creates various records, climbs mountains, jumps, fences, wrestles, fights, and so on. In all these instances, that is, in the work of the thinking center as well as in the work of the emotional and the moving centers, when they work with the energy of

the sex center, there is always one general characteristic and this is a certain particular vehemence and, together with it, the uselessness of the work in question. Neither the thinking nor the emotional nor the moving centers can ever create anything useful with the energy of the sex center. This is an example of the 'abuse of sex.'

When we 'give attention' to the automatic manifestations of the thinking, feeling and moving brains, it inevitably leads to "abuse."

△ △ △

## INSTINCTIVE/SEX CENTERS: THE SURVIVAL TRIADS

Why did Gurdjieff put primary emphasis on Exioëhary as sex energy, rather than on Exioëhary as Attention? We understand that it is because of the following:

> "Can sex be regarded as an independent center?" asked one of those present.
> "It can," said G. "At the same time if all the lower story is taken as one whole, then sex can be regarded as the neutralizing part of the moving center." (*ISM*, P 257)

The illustration of the three Survival triads placed here emphasizes the *essentiality of attention*, which provides the focus, differentiation and creation of patterns which activate/enliven the three brains. Without ~*attention*~ the various brain centers do not participate in the 'present moment' of the event and they thus function, if at all, below the level of consciousness that the particular brain manifests. Here, it is important to remember that each 'hydrogen' category is very large. As a result there will be many attentions each with different levels of vibration (energy) and having different influences on what is focused upon.

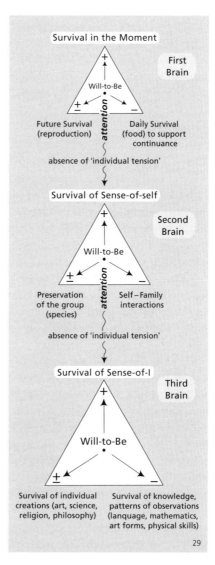

A separated, impartial attention is the highest expression of H12, being able to see, differentiate and create patterns quite aside from those produced by the entrained, partial attentions. It is this highest level of H12, which functions as the Reconciling Force (the plus/minus), the Exioëhary, in the creation of a new physical being and may serve a similar role in the creation of a higher, non-physical body.

### The Will-To-Be — H6

Higher than the H12 category of matter is the Will itself. The particle of Will given to all living beings lies at the center of the survival triads and it is this that empowers the Attentions.

Depending on the assessment of the external sensory systems of the first brain (that there is, or is not, an immediate threat to life, a source of food or a potential mate), the Will-to-be moves into the second and/or third brain triad depending on the ordinary life circumstances. The transition from one brain triad to another can be nearly instantaneous.

### *Examples:*

I am sitting in a barber's chair, about to have a haircut. The hairstylist has turned a radio on and it is broadcasting a constant stream of 'pop' music (which I really do not care for). The hairstylist does not talk (fortunately) but I am aware of the snipping and combing on my scalp. When I sat down, I had the wish and intention to follow my breath throughout the haircut. I focused my attention and quietly began to simply follow the inflow – outflow of my breathing. I was relaxed and episodically sensed my feet and/or shoulders and relaxed any muscular tension found.

Episodically, I note that following the breath is momentarily interrupted by the music (my attention being suddenly and briefly switched to the music) or by the physical sensation of my hair being pulled slightly or now, by the electric razor moving along the edge of my neck. Each of these episodes is brief, perhaps less than a second, and then my attention is back on the breath. The attention on the breath has interesting fluctuations as well– a clear focus on the in-breath, now on the interval between the in- and out-breath and now on the out-breath–and now on the rapid spread of sensation from the end of the out-breath out into the entire body–a very momentary but clear process of 'something' moving out into the body but directly in continuity with the out-breath. Separate from each and all of these points-of-attention, there are several very brief experiences of a 'state of separation' when there is an impartial attention that is clearly aware of the entire process taking place (the in and out breathing, the music, the scalp sensations, sitting in the chair, being in that 'space'). These extremely brief moments are, with a very clear recognition, the most important of all of the qualities of attention that are present during the event.

## *A Second Event:*

The morning preparation, as I was given it, has many forms. They involve complex sensings and/or serial visualizations which can tax (and defeat) the attention in many different ways. The wish to carry through this exercise must be refreshed with some constancy. At the end of one of these preparations was a quite lengthy period of sitting quietly and 'simply' following the breath with a subvocalized "I" on inspiration and a subvocalized "AM" on expiration. During the twenty or so minutes of this practice, a number of changes in the qualities of the attention were notable. The first remembrance is that the quality, or purity, of the attention was on several levels throughout. There were no sounds or touchings to distract, as there were in the first example.

There was a clear separation-of-perception to the in-breath (I), the slight gap or pause between the in-breath and the out-breath (AM), the out-breath (AM) and the 'flow' out into the body. Sometimes the in-breath (I) became a momentary focus of attention (the 'perception' was stronger, more distinct) and, at other times, the out-breath (AM) 'dropped' out of the attention but the focus on the in-out breath continued. At times, the "I–AM" subvocally returned, as if I momentarily remembered that I had forgotten to include them. Remembering this later, I concluded that what was happening was that following the breath required an attention that moved relative to the physical body whereas the subvocalized "I–AM" required an attention that 'moved' through a part of the intellectual center.

What is most notable about the Attention during this morning preparation was the remarkable variation in quality. Throughout, there was a clear, 'spacial' separation from the quiet sitting 'stance' of the body. It was as if this level of attention formed a panorama or 'field' in which other, more delicate or subtle, attentions moved, sometimes with a focus on the in-breath and, at times, on the out-breath or the outward flow into the body. What was also noted was a kind of upward-inward motion on inspiration and a downward (or away-from) motion on expiration. The attention, itself, was 'independent' of these qualitative differences, as if there were multiple attentions moving relative to each other.

Our aim, in this remembrance of the processes taking place during these two events (the haircut and the morning preparation), was to highlight the presence of multiple 'levels' or 'qualities' of attention. This should not be surprising, as the H12 category of matter is very large, and, if it is, as we maintain, of the category that encompasses the photonic energies, it would be extremely (perhaps infinitely) varied in vibratory rates. Photons do not 'interfere' with each other and this makes possible a simultaneity of multiple levels, or qualities, of attention. Perhaps, different parts of aspects of the three brains generate different frequencies of photons, quite specific to a particular function, such that simultaneous but different photonic frequencies are present. A 'noticing' of these different frequencies would be a very different functional expression or level of attention, one that could 'incorporate' or include multiple levels in its perception.

THIRD STRIVING

### The Role of Wish

In a previous segment, we explored the significance Gurdjieff placed on wishing, when it was a true essence wish. We repeat a brief quote here:

> If you "wish" you "can." Without "wishing" you never "can." Wish is the most powerful thing in the world. Higher than God. With conscious wish everything comes.

What a paradoxical thing to say!
From this statement, several questions emerged.

△ Can we wish, really wish from our essence, without an effort being made toward the fulfillment of the wish? Effort is an expression of the Will.

△ Can we really wish if we have not formed a clear, reasonable and conscious notion of what we wish for?

△ Can we really wish if we do not have a feeling of great value for the focus of our wish?

Wish, then, when it is genuine and essence based, includes:

△ our little, inadequate Will,

△ our reason, as best we can understand the complexity and subtleties of our wish and

△ our *value-for* or *love-for* what we wish for.

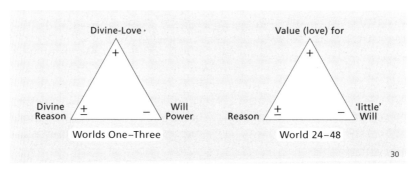

30

This triad of 'forces' (illustration 30) is a World 48–24 'echo' of the primal triad of World One.

Gurdjieff also emphasizes that a real wish must be answered by the entire cosmos. It cannot be denied. Perhaps in this is an approach to understanding Gurdjieff's enigmatic expression, "Higher than God."

---

ENDNOTES, PAGE 16

I  Deutsche, David, *The Beginning of Infinity*, New York: Penguin Books, 2011, P 23.
II  Gurdjieff, *Views from the Real World*, P 197.
III  Deutsche, *The Beginning of Infinity*, P 63.
IV  Gurdjieff, *Views from the Real World*, P 202.

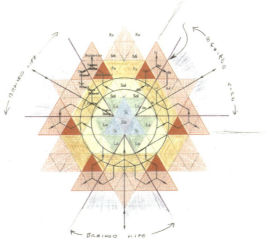

"This [the] lateral octave can give us a glimpse of the source of the evolutionary impulse, which is so difficult to understand within ourselves. And one can say that our reason for existing – the hidden meaning of both our outer and inner movements, of our contradictions as well as our destiny – is all inscribed in us, and nothing could be more important for us that to try to decipher it."*

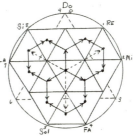

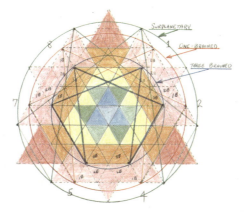

A presentation of the author's drawings and his efforts to study the Laws, "… to fathom the gist …." What emerged, in these early efforts, was a triadic unfolding of our Universe — *A Symbol of the Cosmos and Its Laws*. Its relation to the Law of Heptaparaparshinokh and Triamazikamo is evidenced by these early hand-drawn illustrations.

* Conge, Michel, *Inner Octaves*, P 11.

In Gurdjieff's terms, the inner growth that leads to the creation of a soul capable of serving universal consciousness depends on the uncovering, under all the layers of ego, of conscience. At one point he writes that conscience arises in human beings from the "emanations of the sorrow" of our creator. One can understand this sorrow as arising from the necessary separation of created beings from the creator, a separation required for the development of individual consciousnesses which ultimately can reunite with Him. In each of us this results in a struggle between the needs of the body and the needs of the soul.[I]

D. Wertenbaker

So the plasma, the fourth state of matter could fulfill the criteria needed to be the material of which the soul is composed. It can form entities, is lighter and finer than the body, can interact with its surroundings, and can be of sufficient complexity to support consciousness. Since consciousness supported by the brain seems to depend critically on electromagnetic interactions, perhaps it is even more suited than the brain to support consciousness.[II]

D. Wertenbaker

Man has every possibility, but must earn his way back. Unconscious we are tools of nature. Conscious we become Sons of God, instead of slaves of nature.[III]

J. Heap

I am attention. This body will perish, and these mental constructs will disappear. I am attention; this is my only reality. If this state becomes one of permanent clarity, then it cannot be destroyed. This attention, or this consciousness—which from all eternity has been and remains outside this cycle—is simultaneously present in time. And in this time it is engaged in 'something' it does not become disengaged.[VI]

M. Conge

ENDNOTES, PAGE 125

# Afterword

## " ... AN ORGAN LIKE KUNDABUFFER ... "

The implantation of Kundabuffer, however we come to understand it, was a process that took place in accordance with laws that were an expression from worlds higher than the planet Earth (World 48). We have come to understand these laws as having to do with biological processes involving the world of atoms, ions and molecules. The myth marks this as an event under the direction of the High Commission (the Archangel Sakaki and the Archangel Looisos, the Chief-Common-Universal-Arch-Chemist-Physicist). We understand this to refer to Solar (World 12) and Planetary (World 24) Laws which 'directed' the biological (evolution of life) processes that guided the appearance of life and of brained beings.

In previous volumes we have explored the emergence and development of brained beings, starting from one-brained beings (cold-blooded life-forms with a brain triad ordered by survival in the moment, survival by taking in food, and survival by sexual reproduction). Later (many millions of years later), the second (mammalian, warm-blooded) brain underwent rapid development and aspects of the third brain began to appear.

Throughout the development of brained beings, the survival triad of the first brain retained its dominance and the dependence on the digestion of food, the intake of air and presence of sensory systems continued. All brained life has this enneagrammatic form (illustration 11 on P 57).

# Third Striving

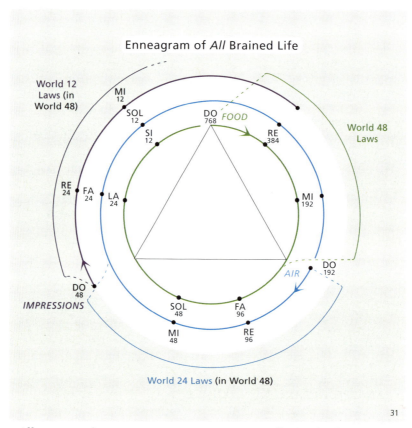

31

All steps in this enneagram occur automatically (under lawful expressions of Worlds 48–24–12).

Three-brained beings (that's us!) have the same enneagrammatic progression. There is no consciousness of any of these processes.

This automatic progression, driven by rigid adherence to biological law, is how we have come to understand Kundabuffer. It is implanted from Above and created the 'topsy-turvy' perception that the world of the physical body (its survival, its need for food, its dependence on sex) was the Reality. The satisfaction of physical desires became, and remains, the focal thrust of this limited perception of Reality.

## FA and RE 96 – SOL and MI 48

The uniqueness of this body is established at FA96. The DNA, which controls this unfolding of the unique protein substances that make up my tissues and organs, is derived from the unique combination of my father's and mother's DNA (a half from each). RE96, on the other hand, is not unique but is the source of activating hormones that are the same in all three-brained beings. The combination (at FA96 and RE96) of chemical substances of self (myself) and other (other 'selves') marks out an essential and pervasive 'arena' of contrast, reconciliation and conflict within each of us–that is in our physical nature. All of this takes place in the non-conscious world of biochemistry.

When elements of a central nervous system begin to appear (the first brain), they serve the preservation of the physical self and the activities (the substrate of feelings) it participates in, via the energizing influence of the hormonal system. Here, the elaboration of thymic, pancreatic, thyroid, adrenal, pituitary and sexual hormones contribute to the plethora of feeling states that serve the body in its interactions with other bodies. Keep in mind that these hormones are identical substances in all three-brained beings—implying that the automatic feeling states will be the same (your anger is the same as my anger; your pleasure is my pleasure; your anxiety is my anxiety) in its biochemical origin.

The sensory aspects of the brain, which are reporting on the internal environment of the body, are immediate reflections of those complex biochemical functions. They report on the meaning of that complex biochemistry in terms of the first-brain survival triad. This is an enormously complex biochemical mix of influences – all of them totally below the level of consciousness.

The external senses of the first brain report, via $DO_{48}$ (in visual, auditory, smell, taste and touch images), on the state of the external world–whether it represents a threat, a source of food or possible mate. The internal senses respond to this external data and prepare and guide the body in its responses to the external world.

One essential point here is that the neural networks that form the core of $SOL_{48}$ and $MI_{48}$ are truly unconscious. From these inputs will be created the images at $LA_{24}$ (physical, emotional and intellectual images) which are essential to the survival and continuity of the body and its arena of relationships with others.

## *In Sum*

This brief discussion of the enneagrammatic, digestive processes is meant to highlight:

△ The entire octave of food ($DO_{768}$ to $SI_{12}$) originates in the unconscious world of the body and passes (at $LA_{24}$) into the subconscious world of the first brain. All of the steps in this process are biochemical-electromagnetic–hence, are automatic.

△ These processes form a quite precise description of Gurdjieff's consideration of Kundabuffer (*BT*, PP 88-89).

## Removal and Destruction of Kundabuffer

"And during just this third descent there, when it was made clear by the thorough investigations of the sacred members of this third Most High Commission that for the maintenance of the existence of those said detached fragments there was no longer any need to continue in actualization of the deliberately taken anticipatory measures, then among the other measures there was also destroyed, with the help of the same Arch-Chemist-Physicist Angel Looisos, in the presences of the three-brained beings there, the said organ Kundabuffer with all its astonishing properties. (BT, P 90)

Gurdjieff often used colorful and dramatic terms to characterize certain changes that are undertaken in *Beelzebub's Tales*. Examples are "to destroy" (Frontispiece) and "to corrode" (BT, P 1184). They are not to be taken literally (in the physical sense) but have a clear psychological (intellectual/emotional) meaning. We understand his use of "destroyed" in the above quotation in the same way–that it is a metaphorical reference to a biological/psychological process. This interpretation of meaning is made more clear by Gurdjieff's reference to "the crystallized consequences of the properties of the organ Kundabuffer." This "organ" continues to function (biologically) in us but via "consequences," because a new process has entered the biological/psychological process which makes it possible to become 'free' of the consequences of the organ itself; that new process is the appearance of an impartial, separated attention (a new level of consciousness). Gurdjieff's detailed description of the first conscious shock is what makes it possible to free man from Kundabuffer although the subconscious, automatic, biological processes still continue– and do so for the remainder of a person's life. In a sense, then, we could say that, while the biologically-based processes, the 'automaton' continue, we can be free of their direct influence in controlling our subconscious life.

The first conscious shock opens to the perspective, as Gurdjieff said, that the subconscious is our true consciousness. The first conscious shock also makes possible the passage of MI$_{48}$ to FA$_{24}$ of the Air Octave—the appearance of consciousness of the images of genuine or real emotion. Keep in mind that the feeling (emotional) images appearing at LA$_{24}$ of the Food Octave are automatic (non-conscious) and become, with the first conscious shock, a source of food to be 'digested' in the development and growth of the Higher Bodies.

### A *New* Organ — *Like* Kundabuffer

The previous segments are preliminary to our core concern in this essay. That concern is focused by the following: (BT, P 1183)

> "THOU ALL and the ALLNESS of my WHOLENESS!
> "The sole means now for the saving of the beings of the planet Earth would be to implant again into their presences a new organ, an organ like Kundabuffer, but this time of such properties that every one of these unfortunates during the process of existence should constantly sense and be cognizant of the inevitability of his own death as well as of the death of everyone upon whom his eyes or attention rests.

> "Only such a sensation and such a cognizance can now destroy the egoism completely crystallized in them that has swallowed up the whole of their Essence and also that tendency to hate others which flows from it—the tendency, namely, which engenders all those mutual relationships existing there, which serve as the chief cause of all their abnormalities unbecoming to three-brained beings and maleficent for them themselves and for the whole of the Universe."

What does "like Kundabuffer" actually mean?
How does this 'implantation' take place?
How to understand "such properties"?
How does "such a cognizance" destroy egoism?

In the opening segment, we explored a biochemical and electromagnetic explanation for the original implantation of Kundabuffer. It is reasonable to apply the same scientifically-based (biochemical-electromagnetic) explanation to the appearance (the implantation) of a new organ.

Just as the original implantation was, in reality, a very complex and extremely long process (encompassing many millions of years), the implantation of a new organ would, by implication, also be a very complex and prolonged process. It would involve changes especially in the electromagnetic arena of brain function (note the reference to "sensation" and "cognize"). The changes being referred to must involve a change in the level of consciousness. The biological lawfulness — that everything dies — must become a conscious and constant product of brained activity.

## Role of Hassein

The noted quotation focuses on the answer Beelzebub gives to HIS ENDLESSNESS but it is essential to have in mind the *set up* to his answer. It is Hassein's question (put in a context or image 'as if' Beelzebub stood before HIS ENDLESSNESS). Gurdjieff's description of Beelzebub's response is critical to note: (*BT*, p 1183)

> Thereupon Beelzebub suddenly also arose unexpectedly and having stretched His right hand forward and His left hand back, He directed His vision somewhere afar off, and it seemed that with His sight He was, as it were, piercing the very depths of space.
>
> Simultaneously 'something' pale yellow began little by little to arise around Beelzebub and to envelop Him, and it was in no way possible to understand or to discern whence this something issued—whether it issued from Beelzebub Himself or proceeded to Him from space from sources outside of Him.
>
> Finding Himself in these cosmic actualizations incomprehensible for all three-brained beings, Beelzebub in a loud voice unusual for Him very penetratingly intoned the following words:
> "THOU ALL and the ALLNESS of my WHOLENESS!

Hassein's question has become HIS ENDLESSNESS' question, because Gurdjieff has suddenly created a scenario in which Beelzebub really does appear in the presence of HIS ENDLESSNESS! It would appear that Hassein's question is also a question for HIS ENDLESSNESS. That HIS ENDLESSNESS did not know the answer as to how best to help the three-brained beings of Earth is important to highlight, as it underscores the role of such cosmic individuals as Beelzebub in the "administration of the enlarging World." There are, therefore, circumstances that lawfully occur, which HIS ENDLESSNESS does not know about. Gurdjieff has also, simultaneously, placed Hassein in the role of fulfilling the task of the implantation of the new organ! This is the nidus of the final segment of *The Tales*.

Who is Hassein? And how are we to understand 'his' responsibility?

Are we (men and women of Work) the grandchildren of Beelzebub?

If we understand our contributing role in this way, what are we to do that could possibly influence the psychological-spiritual future of mankind? Is that a preposterous question?

## Consciousness and the Future

Gurdjieff locates the first conscious shock at the most critical juncture of the three Digestive Octaves. When this takes place at the $DO_{48}$ of Impressions (and, simultaneously, enters into the passage of $MI_{48}$ to $FA_{24}$ of Air, and sees into the automatic images at $LA_{24}$), one begins to become immediately aware of the automatic and, simultaneously, begins the long road to the full 'consciousness of Being'. The awareness of one's physical mortality becomes ever more evident.

## The Destruction of Egoism

From what Gurdjieff has explained at other times, it is our understanding that egoism, at its core, is not destroyed until the passage through the second conscious shock. That passage lies a very great distance from the first conscious shock, requiring a significant portion of at least a lifetime of Work. The first conscious shock is the essential, ongoing effort in this process. The process that Gurdjieff is referring to as the future responsibility of Hassein is obviously a multi-generational one.

Bringing consciousness of a higher quality into the life of mankind is a most formidable challenge, and the challenge must enter into every facet of everyday life.

## Time

In the sixty-some years since Gurdjieff's death there has been a quite remarkable growth of Work groups. There are many thousands of individuals in these groups and, in recent years, there has been an increasing and rapid sharing of experiences, perspectives, methods and emotional support between these groups. There is every reason to believe that this dissemination of Work will continue to penetrate into the broader life of man. The bedrock of this growth is an increase in consciousness of the inner-outer world of life.

△   △   △

## Involution?

There is frequent mention in Work literature of the involution of primal influence ("C" influence) after the death of its originator or Messenger. Gurdjieff alludes to this process often, and many have interpreted the inclusion of "Salzmanino" (*BT*, p 659) as a reflection of this lawful process. What must be remembered, however, is that Gurdjieff has Beelzebub emerge unchanged from his visit to Deskaldino on his way home to Karatas. This could be interpreted, as we do, to mean that Beelzebub — His teaching — emerges from the inevitable and lawful difficulties, the multiple 'comets' with their Zilnotrago that disorganizes the functions of the planetary body until all the 'Zilnotrago' is volatilized out of it, essentially unscathed and proceeds toward Karatas ('the hard stony way to Love').

If we understand the primal thrust of Gurdjieff's teaching as being to make possible the increasing consciousness of all three centers, then the considerable development of groups throughout the world which are in common pursuit of increasing consciousness is an evolutional development.

For us, the hallmark of this evolutional motion lies in the dramatic increase in the study of Gurdjieff's literary, practical and artistic efforts. The study of *Beelzebub's Tales* that is rapidly increasing is especially important, as are the concentrated efforts on Movements and Sacred Dances. Rather than being seen as a lessening or an involution of the primal impulse originating from Gurdjieff, we choose to see these developments as self-correcting efforts to bring his undiluted message of increasing consciousness to a wider and wider segment of humanity. In this way, over perhaps many generations of 'grandchildren', the consciousness of mankind will undergo a real transformation — a true fulfillment of Gurdjieff's essence wish for each of us.

What we are pointing to, in the current and continuing 'motions' between groups that derive, in their origins, from impulses initiated by Ouspensky, de Salzmann, Bennett, Nyland, Staveley, etc., is that what appears to be emerging, slowly and with variable emphases, is a return to the primacy of Gurdjieff's teaching. What we see, on the part of these significant mentors and first generation teacher-mentors, is their interpretations, with varying emphases, of certain aspects of what Gurdjieff brought. None of them could be considered wrong but each of them could be understood as being incomplete. Even if some of the 'interpretations' were considered 'incorrect' in some ways, that would not detract from their essentially helpful message — for which we must have endless gratitude.

What we see when we look at all the literature that has been produced by these remarkable people is a 'representation' of Work which has emphasis on certain aspects, but not others. Each has a significant amount of the subjectivity of these individuals in their 'teaching'. This is how we understand the influence of the cometary 'Zilnotrago'. They are, unfortunately, disharmonizing influences on the 'planetary body's functioning' while we live through them. The 'we' in the last sentence is all of 'us' of the generations that have been led by the first generation of pupils of Gurdjieff.

Through all the 'comets', Beelzebub is still able to get to Deskaldino and be in the presence of the creator of his true Being. We understand this as indicating that the 'heart' of Gurdjieff's teaching is there, surrounded, if you will, by all the 'comets' that are lawful but individually subjective disharmonizing influences on the true whole essence of the teaching. But Beelzebub emerges from Deskaldino intact – whole – and continues into his future destination which is presumptively reached on Karatas.

Hassein also emerges intact – ready to undertake his responsible life. What he retains is what he has learned directly from Beelzebub; his stature, his capacity is recognized by his grandfather. (Remember, his two 'sons' have gone on to fulfill their responsibilities, which are not Hassein's).

We understand that what Gurdjieff is inferring, in this mythic presentation, is that there will be (as we now see in motion) a recollecting (not in memory – but in actuality) of the core message of Gurdjieff. The current and growing study of *The Tales*, movements, inner exercises and group meetings/gatherings are testimony to that motion. Increasingly, while there is appropriate veneration of our varied 'teachers', there is increasing focus on the core of Gurdjieff teachings coming directly from him.

In this way, over perhaps many generations of 'grandchildren', the consciousness of mankind will undergo a real transformation — a true fulfillment of Gurdjieff's essence wish for each of us.

> '... Try to put yourself in the position of others – they have the same significance as you; they suffer as you do, and, like you, they will die. Only if you always try to sense this significance until it becomes a habit whenever your attention rests on anyone, only then will you be able to assimilate the good part of air and have a real "I". Every man has wants and desires which are dear to him, and which he will lose at death.
>
> 'From realizing the significance of your neighbor when your attention rests on him, that he will die, pity for him and compassion towards him will arise in you, and finally you will love him; also, by doing this constantly, real faith, conscious faith, will arise in some part of you and spread to other parts, and you will have the possibility of knowing real happiness, because from this faith objective hope will arise – hope of a basis for continuation.'[1]

1  C. S. Nott, *Teachings of Gurdjieff*, (New York; Penguin, 1991), p 114.

# Involution?

Understanding the nature of the world and our place in it has always been the goal of both the study of the external world and the inner search for meaning, but in modern times these two approaches become artificially separated, almost as if to give the powerful methodology of science a chance to develop. Now, however, it seems time for attempts at reunification.[2]

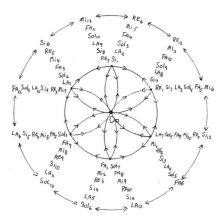

Can we nevertheless define some possible requirements for consciousness? Each of the following propositions can be and has been disagreed with, but they are not unreasonable. First, for there to be consciousness, there must be an entity that is aware, distinct from what it is aware of; and conversely, it must be in some kind of communication with what it is aware of. Second, such an entity must have sufficient complexity to both maintain itself–for a time–as an entity, and to apprehend externals. In us, the senses and the brain that analyses them fulfill the latter function and contribute to the former. Third, the entity must be capable of change, growth, or learning; therefore it must have a memory.[3]

---

2 Wertenbaker, *Man in the Cosmos*, p 101.
3 Ibid., pp 115-16.

---

ENDNOTES, PAGE 116
  I Wertenbaker, *Man in the Cosmos*, p 145.
  II Ibid., p 129.
  III Jane Heap
  IV Conge, *Inner Octaves*, p 66.

△ △ △

# Glossary

ATOM–a tiny basic building block of matter. All the material on Earth is composed of various combinations of atoms.

ATOMIC TABLE OF THE ELEMENTS (The Periodic Table)–is a tabular display of the chemical elements, organized on the basis of their properties.

ATTENTION(S)—a photonic power having a tripartite nature, the capacity to: focus–*creating* 1s, differentiate–*creating* 2s, and form patterns–*creating* 3s.

AXIS/AXIES–one, two or more lines on which coordinates are measured.

AXONS–an extension of a nerve cell, similar in shape to a thread, that transmits impulses outward from the cell body.

BIOCHEMICAL–chemicals that are active in living systems.

BIOPHOTON–roles played by photons in living systems.

BONDS (crystalline, interatomic, hydrogen)–varying types of interatomic electronic energies that hold atoms together.

BUTTERFLY EFFECT–a term used in chaos theory to describe how small changes to a seemingly unrelated thing or condition (also known as an initial condition) can affect large, complex systems.

CELL MEMBRANES–coalescence of substances that form the exterior coating of the cell.

CENTRAL NERVOUS SYSTEM–the part of the nervous system, consisting of the brain and spinal cord, that controls and coordinates most functions of the body and mind.

CHARGED ATOM–an atom with more, or fewer, electrons in orbit; an ion.

CHEMICAL BONDS–the force resulting from the distribution of energy contained by orbiting electrons, which tends to bind atoms together to form molecules.

COVALENT–a chemical bond between two atoms created by the sharing of a pair of electrons.

CELL NUCLEI–special organelle containing the DNA.

DNA–a nucleic acid molecule in the form of a twisted double strand (double helix) that is the major component of chromosomes and carries genetic information.

ELECTROMAGNETIC–created by or relating to electromagnetism.

ELECTROMAGNETIC SPECTRUM–the complete range of electromagnetic radiation from the shortest waves (Gamma rays) to the longest (radio and ELF waves).

ELECTRON–a stable, negatively charged elementary particle with a small mass that is a fundamental constituent of matter and may orbit the nucleus of an atom.

ELECTRON ORBITALS–the pathways of an electron around an atomic nucleus.

ELF–extremely low frequency of electromagnetic waves–extending from 0.1 to 100 vibrations per second. This corresponds to wavelengths of hundreds of thousands of miles.

ENZYME–a complex protein produced by living cells that promotes a specific biochemical reaction by acting as a catalyst.

$E=MC^2$ –mathematical formula expressing the equivalence of energy and mass (E = energy; M = mass; C = speed of light in a vacuum).

EXTERNAL SENSES–any of the six agencies by which an individual receives impressions of the outside world through taste, touch, smell, hearing, sight or balance.

GAMMA WAVE–the shortest wavelengths of electromagnetic radiation.

GLUON–a theoretical elementary particle without mass, thought to be involved in binding the subatomic particles together.

HORMONE–a chemical substance produced in the body's endocrine glands or certain other cells that exerts a regulatory or stimulatory effect in metabolism.

INFRARED WAVE–the portion of the invisible electromagnetic spectrum consisting of radiation with wavelengths between visible light and radio waves.

INTERCELLULAR–biological processes existing between cells.

IONIC WAVE–relating to charged atoms or groups of charged atoms which undergo successive depolarization.

ION–charged atom.

MATTER–the material substances of the Universe that have mass and are convertible to energy.

MICROWAVE–a type of electromagnetic wave whose wavelength ranges from radio waves to infrared waves.

MORPHOGENESIS–the process which explains how living beings take form or shape.

NEOCORTEX / NEOCORTICAL BRAIN–the brain of intellectual capacities (referred to as the "third brain").

NEURON– a grayish or reddish granular cell with specialized processes that is the fundamental functional unit of nervous tissue.

NEUROPEPTIDE–a small protein-like substance active in neural systems.

NEUROTRANSMITTERS–a chemical that carries messages between different nerve cells or between nerve cells and muscles, usually to trigger or prevent an impulse in the receiving cell.

NEUTRON–a neutrally-charged elementary particle.

NUCLEAR MEMBRANE–membrane surrounding the nucleus of the cell.

ONTIC–describes what is there, as opposed to the nature or properties of a being.

OVUM–a female reproductive cell or gamete.

PARASYMPATHETIC–that small portion of the parasympathetic nervous system which is located in the lower-most segment of the spinal cord. It is the 'final common pathway' of control for the last portion of the colon, the bladder and the sexual reproductive organs.

PARTICLE/WAVE DUALITY–meaning simultaneously, in their nature, both particle-like and wave-like, the fundamental concept of quantum mechanics that holds that light and elementary particles have a dual nature.

PERIODIC TABLE OF THE ELEMENTS OR THE ATOMIC TABLE–is a tabular display (in order of the atomic number) of the chemical elements, organized on the basis of their properties.

PHOTON–a quantum of visible light or other form of electromagnetic radiation demonstrating both particle and wave properties.

PLASMA STATE–a state of high matter/energy similar to gas in which a certain portion of the particles are ionized.

PROTON–a positively-charged elementary particle.

QUANTUM THEORY–theory developed by Max Planck that maintained the unitary emission of energy. The theory was further expanded by scientists of the early 20th century.

QUARK–an elementary particle with an electric charge equal to one-third or two-thirds of the electron. Quarks are believed to be the constituents of baryons and mesons.

RADIOACTIVITY–radiation; the high-energy particles emitted by radioactive substances.

RESONANT REPRESENTATION–an image produced by the brain.

STRONG NUCLEAR FORCE–the fundamental force binding the nuclei of an atom together.

ULTRAVIOLET–electromagnetic radiation of wavelengths higher than the violet end of the visible light spectrum and lower than the gamma spectrum.

WEAK NUCLEAR FORCE–the fundamental force mediating the decay of the nucleus of an atom.

X-RAY–a high-energy EM radiation lying between ultraviolet and gamma waves.

△   △   △

# Recommended Reading — References

Alexandrov, B. S., V. Gelev, A. R. Bishop, A. Usheva, K. O. Rasmussen.
"DNA Breathing Dynamics in the Presence of a Terahertz Field,"
*Physics Letters A* volume 374, issue 10, 2010.

Barrow, John.
*Theories of Everything: The Quest for Ultimate Explanation.*
New York: Ballantine Books, 1992.

Bennett, John G.
*An Introduction to "Life is Real only then, when 'I am'"*
Sherborne: Coombe Springs Press, 1975.
*Deeper Man.* Santa Fe: Bennett Books, 1995.
*Energies: Material, Vital and Cosmic.* Sherbourne:
Coombe Springs Press, 1964.
*Enneagram Studies.* Kennebunkport: Samuel Weiser, 1983.
*Gurdjieff: Making a New World.* New York: Harper & Row, 1973.
*Hazard.* Santa Fe: Bennett Books, 1991.
*J. G. Bennett's Talks on Beelzebub's Tales.* York Beach: Weiser, 1988.
*Making a Soul: Human Destiny and the Debt of Our Existence.*
Santa Fe: Bennett Books, 1995.
*The Crisis in Human Affairs.* New York: Heritage House, 1951.
*The Dramatic Universe.* Charles Town: Claymont Communications, 1987.
*The Masters of Wisdom.* Santa Fe: Bennett Books, 1995.
*Transformation.* Santa Fe: Bennett Books, 2003.

Bischof, Marco.
*Biophotons - The Light in Our Cells.* Frankfurt: Zweitausendeins, 1998.

Bohm, David.
*The Ending of Time.* New York: Harper & Row, 1980.
*Wholeness and the Implicate Order.* And Jiddu Krishnamurti. London:
Routledge, Keegan and Paul, 1980.
*The Essential Bohm.* ed. Lee Nichol. New York: Routledge, 2003.

Bohr, Niels.
*The Philosophical Writings of Niels Bohr,*
Volume 2. Woodbridge: Ox Bow Press, 1987.

Bowler, Peter.
  *Reconciling Science and Religion: the Debate in Early Twentieth Century Britain.* Chicago: University of Chicago Press, 2001.

Buzzell, Keith A.
  *Children of Cyclops: Neurophysiology of Television Viewing.* Fair Oaks: AWSNA Publications, 2003.
  *Perspectives on Beelzebub's Tales.* Salt Lake City: Fifth Press, 2005.
  *Explorations in Active Mentation.* Salt Lake City: Fifth Press, 2006.
  *Man – A Three-Brained Being.* Salt Lake City: Fifth Press, 2007.
  *Reflections on Gurdjieff's Whim,* Salt Lake City: Fifth Press, 2012.
  *A New Conception of God: Further Reflections of Gurdjieff's Whim* Salt Lake City: Fifth Press, 2013

Calaprice, Alice, editor.
  *The New Quotable Einstein.* Princeton: Princeton University Press, 2000.

Capra, Fritjof. *The Tao of Physics.* Boston: Shambhala, 1991.
  *Uncommon Wisdom: Conversations with Remarkable People.* New York: Bantam Books, 1988.

Campbell, Joseph.
  *Creative Mythology.* New York: Penguin Viking Books, 1968.
  *The Masks of God, (4 volumes).* New York: Penguin Arkana, 1959, 62, 64, 68(1991).
  *The Hero with the Thousand Faces.* Novato: New World Library, 2008.

Cantor, George.
  *Contributions to the Founding of the Theory of Transfinite Numbers.* Philip Jourdain, ed. and trans. New York, Dover, Books 1955.

Changeux, Jean-Pierre.
  Chemical Signaling in the Brain. *Scientific American* (November 1993), 58-62.

Cirlot, J. A.
  *Dictionary of Symbols.* New York: Philosophical Library, 1962.

Cooper, Jack, R., Floyd E. Bloom, Robert H. Roth.
  *The Biochemical Basis of Neuropharmacology.* New York: Oxford University Press, 1991.

Conge, Michel.
  *Inner Octaves.* Toronto: Dolmen Meadow Editions, 2007.

Copley, Frank O. translater.
  *Lucretius: The Nature of Things.* New York: W. W. Norton & Co., 1977

Dalai Lama, H.H.
  *The Universe in a Single Atom: The Convergence of Science and Spirituality.* New York: Morgan Road Books, 2005.

# Recommended Reading

Damasio, Antonio.
*The Feeling of What Happens.* New York: Harcourt Inc., 1999.

DeArmond, Stephen T., Madeline M. Fusco and Maynard M. Dewey.
*Structure of the Human Brain.* New York: Oxford University Press, 1989.

DeDuve, Christian.
*Vital Dust, Life as a Cosmic Imperative.* New York: Basic Books, 1995.

de Hartmann, Thomas and Olga.
*Our Life with Mr. Gurdjieff.* Definitive Edition, London: Arkana, 1983.

de Salzmann, Jeanne.
"The First Initiation," *Gurdjieff: Essays and Reflections on the Man and His Teaching.* editors. Jacob Needleman and George Baker.
New York: Continuum Press, 1996.
*The Reality of Being.* Boston: Shambhala Publications, 2010.

Dennett, Daniel.
*Freedom Evolves.* New York: Viking Press, 2003.

Einstein, Albert.
*Out of My Later Years.* New York: Philosophical Library, 1950.

Erickson, Milton with Ernest L. Rossi.
*Hypnotic Realities.* New York: Irvington Publishers, 1976.

Ferris, Timothy.
*Coming of Age in the Milky Way.* New York: Harper Collins Anchor, 1989.

Feynman, Richard P.
"The Character of Physical Law," transcript, November, 1964.
*The Pleasure of Finding Things Out: The Best Short Works of Richard P. Feynman.* New York City: Basic Books Perseus Publishing, 1999.

Ginsburg, Seymour.
*Gurdjieff Unveiled: An Overview and Introduction to the Teaching,*
London: Lighthouse Editions, 2005.
*The Masters Speak: An American Businessman Encounters Ashish and Gurdjieff.* Wheaton: Quest Books, 2010.
*In Search of the Unitive Vision.* Boca Raton: New Paradigm Books, 2001.
*What Is Man? Selected Writings of Sri Madhava Ashish.*
New Delhi: Penguin Books, 2010.

Greene, Brian.
*The Fabric of the Cosmos.* New York: Vintage Books, 2004.

*Guide and Index to G.I. Gurdjieff's Beelzebub's Tales to His Grandson.*
Louise M. Welch, editor. Toronto: Traditional Studies Press, 2003.

Gurdjieff, George Ivanovitch.
- "*An Objectively Impartial Criticism of the Life of Man*" or "*Beelzebub's Tales to His Grandson,*" *All and Everything/First Series.*
  Facsimile republication. Aurora: Two Rivers Press, 1993 and the 1999 London: Penguin Arkana edition.
- *Meetings with Remarkable Men, All and Everything/Second Series.*
  New York: Penguin Books, 1991.
- *Life is real only then, when "I am," All and Everything/Third Series.*
  New York: Penguin Books, 1999.
- *Views from the Real World: Early Talks of Gurdjieff.* New York: Penguin Books, 1991.

Harris, Sam.
- *The End of Faith.* New York: W. W. Norton, 2004.

Heap, Jane.
- *The Notes of Jane Heap.* Aurora: Two Rivers Press, 1994.
- *Notes.* Aurora: Two Rivers Press, 1983.

Heyneman, Martha.
- *The Breathing Cathedral.* San Francisco: Sierra Club, 1993.

Hooper, Judith and Dick Teresi.
- *The 3-Pound Universe.* New York: MacMillan Co., 1986.

Hunter, John
- *World Peace and Other 4th-Grade Achievements.* New York: Eamon Dolan/Houghton Mifflin Harcourt, 2013.

Jung, Carl G.
- *Man and His Symbols.* Garden City: Doubleday, 1964.

King, C. Daly.
- *The Oragean Version.* New York: privately printed, 1951.

Krishnamurti, Jiddu and David Bohm.
- *Wholeness and the Implicate Order.*
  London: Routledge, Keegan and Paul, 1980.

Krishnamurti, Jiddu.
- *Krishnamurti to Himself: His Last Journal.*
  New York: HarperCollins, 1993.

Lederman, Leon M.
- *The God Particle.* N Y: First Mariner Books, 2006

Leeming, David and Margaret.
- *A Dictionary of Creation Myths.* N Y: Oxford University Press, 1994.

Malin, Shimon.
- *Nature Loves to Hide.* New York: Oxford University Press, 2001.

# Recommended Reading

MacLean, Paul D.
*The Triune Brain in Evolution.* New York: Plenum Press, 1990.

Mairet, Philip.
*A. R. Orage: a Memoir.* New Hyde Park: University Books, 1966.

McCorkle, Anna Beth.
*The Gurdjieff Years, 1929–1949: Recollections of Louise March.* Utrecht: Eureka Editions, 2012.

McFadden, Johnjoe.
*Quantum Evolution.* London: W. W. Norton, 2000.

Moyzis, Robert K.
"The Human Telomere." *Scientific American* (August 1991), 48-55.

Murchie, Guy.
*The Seven Mysteries of Life.* Boston: Houghton Mifflin Co., 1978.

Needleman, Jacob.
*What is God?* New York: Tarcher/Penguin, 2009.
*The Essential Marcus Aurelius.* translator with John P. Piazza. New York: Tarcher/Penguin, 2008.
*Gurdjieff: Reflections on the Man and His Teaching.* editors, Needleman and Baker. New York: Continuum Press, 1996.

Nicolescu, Basarab.
*Gurdjieff: Essays and Reflections on the Man and His Teaching,* "Gurdjieff's Philosophy of Nature." New York: Continuum Press, 1996.

Nichol, Lee, editor.
*The Essential David Bohm.* New York: Routledge, 2003.

Nicoll, Maurice.
*Psychological Commentaries on the Teaching of G.I. Gurdjieff and P.D. Ouspensky.* York Beach: Weiser, 1996.

Nott, C. S.,
*Journey through this World: The Second Journal of a Pupil.* New York: Weiser, 1969.
*Teachings of Gurdjieff.* New York: Penguin 1991.

Orage, A. R.
*A. R. Orage's Commentaries on G. I. Gurdjieff's All and Everything: Beelzebub's Tales to His Grandson.* C.S. Nott, editor. Aurora: Two Rivers Press, 1985.

Ouspensky, P. D.
*In Search of the Miraculous.* San Diego: Harvest/HBJ Book, 2001.
*A Further Record.* London and New York: Arkana, 1986.,

Pearce, Joseph Chilton.
   *The Biology of Transcendence*. Rochester: Norton Publishers, 2002.
   *Evolution's End: Changing the Potential of Our Intelligence*.
      San Francisco: Harper, 1992.

Peat, F. David.
   *Infinite Potential: The Life and Times of David Bohm*.
   Ann Arbor: University of Michigan Press, 1997.

Popoff, Irmis B.
   *The Enneagramma and the Man of Unity*.
      New York: Red Wheel/Weiser, 1978.
   *Gurdjieff Group Work with Willem Nyland*. York Beach: Weiser, 1983.
   *Gurdjieff: His Work on Myself, With Others, For the Work*.
      New York: Vantage Press, 1969.

Popp, Fritz-Allen.
   "On the coherence of ultraweak photon emissions from living tissues,"
   *Disequilibrium and Self-Organization*. C. W. Kilmister, (ed.), 1986.

Prigogine, Ilya.
   *The End of Certainty*. New York: The Free Press, 1996.

Prigogine, Ilya, E. Stengers.
   *Order Out of Chaos*. New York: Bantam, 1984.

Reiss, Diana.
   *The Dolphin in the Mirror*. Boston: Mariner Books , 2011.

Rudwin, Maximilian.
   *The Devil in Legend and Literature,* 2nd Edition.
   New York: Ams Pr Inc, 1980.

Sandford, Joseph A.
   "Gnosis through Hypnosis: The Role of Trance in Personal
   Transformation." Proceedings of the 10th All & Everything
   International Humanities Conference, 2005.

Smoley, Richard.
   *Inner Christianity: A Guide to the Esoteric Tradition*. Boston:
   Shambhala Publications, 2002.

Staveley, A. L.
   *Themes I*. Aurora: Two Rivers Press, 1981.
   *Memories of Gurdjieff*, Aurora: Two Rivers Press, 1978.

Taylor, Paul Beekman.
   *Shadows of Heaven: Gurdjieff and Toomer*. York Beach: Weiser, 1998,
   *Gurdjieff and Orage: Brothers in Elysium*. York Beach: Weiser, 2001.
   *Gurdjieff's Invention of America,* revised.
      Utrecht: Eureka Editions, 2007.

*The Philosophy of G. I. Gurdjieff: Time, Word and Being in "All and Everything."* Utrecht: Eureka Editions, 2007.

Tcheslaw, Tchekhovitch.
*Gurdjieff A Master in Life.*
Toronto: Dolmen Meadow Editions, 2006.

Tracol, Henri.
*George Ivanovich Gurdjieff: Man's Awakening and the Practice of Remembering Oneself.* London: Pembridge Design Studio Press, 1987.

Welch, Louise M.
*Orage with Gurdjieff in America.*
Boston: Routledge & Kegan Paul, Ltd., 1982.

Weber, Renee.
*Dialogues with Scientists and Sages: The Search for Unity.*
London: Routledge & Kegan Paul, 1986.

Wertenbaker, Christian.
*Man in the Cosmos: G. I. Gurdjieff and Modern Science.*
New Paltz: Codhill Press Books, 2012

Whitehead, Alfred North.
*An Introduction to Mathematics.*
New York: Oxford University Press, 1959.

Young, Arthur M.
*The Geometry of Meaning.* New York: Delacorte Press, 1976.
*The Reflexive Universe.* New York: Delacorte Press, 1976.

Zukov, Gary.
*The Dancing Wu Li Masters.* New York: HarperCollins, 2001.

Reliable websites and links for research of Gurdjieff and his Work:
http://www.gurdjieff.org/
http://gurdjieff-heritage-society.org/
http://jgbftalksandlectures.com/
http://gurdjieff-leeds.org/g-i-gurdjieff/a-r-orage
http://www.gurdjieffbooksandmusic.com/
http://www.bythewaybooks.com/cgi-bin/btw455/index.html
https://www.watkinsbooks.com/

While citing addresses can be subject to the instability of the internet, there are many interesting and useful videos on YouTube from which, for a carefully discriminating person, an image of Gurdjieff and his Work begins to emerge. The subjects include Movements, music, lectures and documentaries.

Documentaries:
http://www.youtube.com/watch?v=mrvy2qYpPI8
http://www.youtube.com/watch?v=LFfa8Ae1Qog&list=PLF451C318F21771DA
http://www.youtube.com/watch?v=X0xMSUyYHPQ&list=PL6270DA62D4F1DF18

### Keith A. Buzzell, A.B., D.O.

Dr. Buzzell was born in 1932 in Boston, Massachusetts. He studied music at Bowdoin College and Boston University and received his medical doctorate in 1960 at the Philadelphia College of Osteopathic Medicine. Dr. Buzzell served as a hospital medical director, a professor of osteopathic medicine and was the founder of the Western Maine hospice program. He has lectured widely on the neuro-physiological influences of television on the developing human brain and on the evolution of man's triune brain. For the past thirty eight years, he has been a rural family physician in Fryeburg, Maine, a staff member of Bridgton Hospital and currently holds the position of medical director at the Fryeburg Health Care Center.

In 1971, Keith and his wife, Marlena, became students of Irmis Popoff, who herself was a student of both Gurdjieff and Ouspensky. She founded the Pinnacle Group in Sea Cliff, Long Island, New York, and from then until the mid 1980s, Keith and Marlena formed Work groups under her supervision. It was in 1988 when they met Annie Lou Staveley, founder of Two Rivers Farm in Oregon, and they maintained a Work relationship with Mrs. Staveley up to her death.

Keith has given presentations at the All and Everything International Humanities Conferences 1996-2003, 2007, 2009, 2012 that have been published in the annual Conference Proceedings (www.aandeconference.org). Keith and Marlena live and continue group Work in Bridgton, Maine.

## Acknowledgements

Cover: 30 Doradus in Ultraviolet, visible and red light: NASA, ESA, F. Paresce (INAF-IASF, Bologna, Italy), R. O'Connell (University of Virginia, Charlottesville), and the Wide Field Camera 3 Science Oversight Committee.

Book design, illustrations: Amy O'Donnell and Michael Hall, under the direction of Keith Buzzell and Bonnie Phillips, editors and the input from many others who contributed their ideas.

Production and proofing: Stephen Seko, Amy O'Donnell, Toddy Smyth and Michael Hall.

Steve Bruun: printing

And, a sincere "thank you" to those (our friends in groups throughout Europe and North America) who assisted in reading and discussing the ideas presented in this book.

## Colophon

This book was set in New Caledonia designed by William A. Dwiggins, issued in digital form by Linotype, Bad Homburg, Germany in 1982. Text for illustrations is set in Frutiger and New Caledonia. Frutiger was designed by Adrian Frutiger, issued by D. Stempel A.G. in conjunction with Linotype Library in 1976. The paper is Mohawk VIA Cool White, seventy pound, one hundred percent post consumer waste.

△   △   △